What to Say When You Talk to AI

Prompt Engineering Guide

By

Susie Hala

Legal Assurance Note

This publication has been fully authored and edited by Susie Hala.
All writing, concepts, and educational interpretations are original and protected under U.S. copyright law.
Any AI tools mentioned or used in the creative process were applied solely for educational illustration.
No part of this work infringes upon the rights, trademarks, or intellectual property of others.

For permissions, inquiries, or bulk purchases, please contact:
Hala Learning Press
Email: halaprosper1@gmail.com

ISBN 979-8-9991963-4-7
Printed in the United States of America

Cover Design © 2025 Hala Learning Press
Author: **Susie Hala**

Disclaimer

This publication is intended to educate and inspire readers about prompt engineering and effective AI communication. It is provided for informational purposes only and does not constitute professional, legal, or technical advice. Readers should apply their own discretion and seek expert guidance when making decisions based on the material presented.

The author and publisher make no guarantees regarding the accuracy, completeness, or reliability of the content or examples. The author and publisher shall not be held liable for any damages or losses arising directly or indirectly from the use of information contained within this book.

All trademarks, logos, product names, and service marks mentioned in this book are the property of their respective owners. References to these brands or technologies are used strictly for educational illustration and do not imply endorsement.

Author’s Rights & Use of AI Tools

Dedication

To every curious mind learning to speak the language of AI —
may your words build bridges between imagination and intelligence.

To educators, dreamers, and creators who believe that communication is the key to every new discovery —
this book is for you.

And to my beloved family, whose love, patience, and encouragement remind me that true intelligence begins with the heart. ❤

— **Susie Hala**

TABLE OF CONTENTS:

🎯 20 AI Tools That Cut Your Workload in Half

Custom Edition by Susie Hala
Author of "What to Say When You Talk to AI"

🧠 Conversational AI Assistants

Your primary thinking partners for writing, research, and problem-solving

1. **ChatGPT (OpenAI)** – Your all-in-one writing, coding, and brainstorming assistant. Great for research, summarization, and idea generation.
2. **Claude (Anthropic)** – Specializes in long-form, thoughtful writing. Perfect for authors, teachers, and professionals.
3. **Gemini 2.5 Pro (Google)** – Integrates directly with Docs, Sheets, and Gmail to simplify writing and research.
4. **Grok (xAI)** – A witty and conversational chatbot by Elon Musk's xAI that combines reasoning with humor.

✍️ Writing & Content Creation Tools

Enhance your writing, generate copy, and refine your message

5. **GrammarlyGO** – Enhances tone, grammar, and creativity while maintaining your natural voice.
6. **CopyAI** – Generates marketing copy, social posts, and product descriptions in seconds.
7. **Copilot (Microsoft)** – Integrated into Word, Excel, and PowerPoint to automate writing and analysis.

🔍 Research & Information Discovery

Find accurate information fast with AI-powered search and analysis

8. **Perplexity AI** – The ultimate AI search and research companion with cited sources.
9. **Elicit** – Summarizes academic papers and helps researchers extract key findings fast.
10. **Techpresso** – A newsletter that delivers the day's most important AI and tech updates in minutes.

Image & Visual Creation

Transform ideas into stunning visuals without design skills

11. **Midjourney** – Transforms text prompts into artistic images and digital designs.
12. **Firefly (Adobe)** – Creates, edits, and enhances visuals with simple text commands.

Video & Motion Content

Create professional videos from text descriptions

13. **Sora (OpenAI)** – Generates lifelike videos from text prompts for marketing and storytelling.

Voice & Audio Production

Professional audio creation for podcasts, videos, and content

14. **ElevenLabs** – Produces realistic voices for audiobooks, podcasts, or videos.
15. **Voicemod** – Changes and enhances your voice in real time for content creation and entertainment.

Music & Sound Design

Compose original music and audio from text descriptions

16. **Suno AI** – Converts words into fully produced songs or background tracks.

Automation & Custom AI Solutions

Build your own AI assistants and automate complex workflows

17. **Manus AI** – A personal AI assistant that automates voice tasks, notes, and daily summaries.
18. **AgentGPT** – Builds and launches your own AI agents that plan, research, and execute tasks.

Developer & Advanced Tools

Open-source and specialized AI for custom applications

19. **Llama 3 (Meta)** – An open-source model for developers to build private or custom AI systems.
20. **DeepSeek** – China's leading AI for multilingual understanding and advanced analysis.

📌 Quick Reference Guide

For Writing: ChatGPT, Claude, GrammarlyGO, CopyAI, Copilot
For Research: Perplexity AI, Elicit, Gemini, Techpresso
For Visuals: Midjourney, Firefly
For Video: Sora
For Audio: ElevenLabs, Voicemod, Suno AI
For Automation: Manus AI, AgentGPT
For Developers: Llama 3, DeepSeek
For Conversation: ChatGPT, Claude, Gemini, Grok

💡 How to Use This Guide

Choose by Task:

- Need to write content? Start with ChatGPT or Claude
- Need visuals? Go to Midjourney or Firefly
- Need research? Use Perplexity AI or Elicit

Choose by Skill Level:

- **Beginners:** ChatGPT, Gemini, GrammarlyGO, Midjourney
- **Intermediate:** Claude, Perplexity AI, Copilot, ElevenLabs
- **Advanced:** AgentGPT, Llama 3, DeepSeek

Choose by Integration:

- **Google Workspace:** Gemini 2.5 Pro
- **Microsoft Office:** Copilot
- **Creative Cloud:** Firefly

All tools listed are as of October 2025. Features, pricing, and availability may change. Visit each tool's official website for the most current information.

🧩 The Bit and Byte Family

Definition and Overview

The **Bit and Byte Family** forms the digital DNA of every computer system — the foundation upon which all programming, AI models, and data storage are built.
A **bit** (short for *binary digit*) is the smallest possible unit of digital information. It can hold one of two values: **0 or 1**, representing *off/on* or *false/true*.

When multiple bits are grouped together, they form **bytes**, **kilobytes**, **megabytes**, and beyond — a structured hierarchy that allows machines to represent everything from numbers and letters to photos, videos, and artificial intelligence models.

In simple terms:

Bits are like individual letters.
Bytes are like words.
Larger data units are like sentences, paragraphs, and books that computers can read.

This binary language is the silent conversation between humans and machines — the bridge between electrical signals and digital understanding. Every AI model, every chat, every image, and even every word in this book is made possible by this family of data units.

⚙️ Why It Matters in AI and Prompt Engineering

When you communicate with an AI model, you're indirectly working with billions — sometimes trillions — of bits and bytes.

- Your *prompts* are converted into numerical representations (tokens), which are sequences of bits.
- The *AI's responses* are computed, stored, and transmitted as bytes.
- Even *model weights* — the learned "memory" of an AI — are measured in gigabytes or terabytes.

Understanding this family helps readers appreciate how language is converted into electrical patterns and stored as data inside vast neural architectures.

🧠 Key Insight for Readers

Think of the Bit and Byte Family as the **alphabet of machines**.
If prompt engineering is the art of speaking to AI, then bits and bytes are the *sound waves* that carry your words to the machine's ears.

The Bit and Byte Family Tree

Member	Abbreviation	Size (Approx.)	Meaning / Example	Used For
Bit	`b`	1 binary value	Smallest unit of data (0 or 1)	Representing logical states (true/false, on/off)
Nibble	—	4 bits	Half a byte (rarely used term but important)	Hexadecimal representation (0–F)
Byte	`B`	8 bits	Smallest addressable unit in memory	Storing a single character (e.g., "A")

Member	Abbreviation	Size (Approx.)	Meaning / Example	Used For
Kilobyte	`KB`	1,024 bytes	About one paragraph of text	Small files, metadata
Megabyte	`MB`	1,024 KB	About a short book	Images, documents
Gigabyte	`GB`	1,024 MB	Around 230 songs or 2 hours of HD video	Software, model weights
Terabyte	`TB`	1,024 GB	Roughly 500 hours of movies	Data storage drives, training datasets
Petabyte	`PB`	1,024 TB	Massive data collections	AI training corpora, research archives
Exabyte	`EB`	1,024 PB	Global-scale digital data	Internet traffic, cloud storage
Zettabyte	`ZB`	1,024 EB	Almost the entire global digital footprint	Global data analytics, cloud AI systems
Yottabyte	`YB`	1,024 ZB	Theoretical maximum — beyond current storage	Future large-scale AI and quantum data

🌍 Analogy for Everyday Readers

If you think of information as water:

- A **bit** is a single drop.
- A **byte** is a spoonful.
- A **megabyte** is a glass.
- A **terabyte** is a swimming pool.
- A **yottabyte** is an entire ocean of digital information.

Each level represents a deeper scale of capacity — and in AI, these digital oceans are where our models *learn, think, and evolve.*

💬 Quick Takeaway

Every AI thought begins as a single bit — and every masterpiece of machine intelligence is built from countless bytes working in harmony.

⚛ The Qubit Family

Definition and Overview

The **Qubit Family** (short for *quantum bit*) represents the next generation of digital intelligence — a revolutionary leap from the classical *bit*.
While a bit can exist only as a **0 or 1**, a **qubit** can exist as **both 0 and 1 at the same time**, thanks to the quantum principle of **superposition**.

This unique property allows quantum computers to perform multiple calculations simultaneously, processing vast combinations of data at once — a feat impossible for traditional systems.

In other words:

If bits are switches that can be "on" or "off," qubits are *waves* that can be "on," "off," or anything in between — all at the same moment.

Quantum computing redefines how we process, store, and use information. For AI and prompt engineering, it hints at a future where machine reasoning could become exponentially faster, more complex, and more energy-efficient.

Why It Matters in AI and Prompt Engineering

Large language models (LLMs) and AI systems today run on classical computers powered by bits and bytes. But researchers are already developing **quantum-enhanced models** that could dramatically increase computational speed and reduce training costs. Qubits open the door to:

- Faster optimization and simulation in AI algorithms
- Exponentially larger search spaces for data analysis
- Quantum-based encryption and security models
- Quantum machine learning (QML) — blending neural networks with quantum mechanics

When this technology matures, the relationship between **prompts, probabilities, and reasoning** will evolve again — allowing AI to explore infinite possibilities simultaneously instead of one outcome at a time.

Key Insight for Readers

Think of qubits as the **dreamers of the digital world** — able to hold contradictions, possibilities, and probabilities in balance.
Prompt engineers of tomorrow will likely need to think *quantumly* — phrasing requests that account for parallel reasoning and multi-dimensional responses.

The Qubit Family Tree

Member	Symbol / Abbreviation	Quantum Concept	Explanation	Used For
Qubit	`	ψ⟩`	**Superposition**	Can represent both 0 and 1 simultaneously
Entangled Qubits	—	**Entanglement**	Two or more qubits linked so that one's	Secure communication, teleportation

Member	Symbol / Abbreviation	Quantum Concept	Explanation	Used For
			state instantly affects the other	
Quantum Register	—	**State Vector**	A collection of qubits storing multi-dimensional data	Quantum computing memory
Quantum Gate	`H, X, Y, Z`	**Quantum Logic Operation**	Manipulates qubits (like logic gates in classical computing)	Quantum algorithms and processing
Quantum Circuit	—	**Quantum Flow**	A sequence of gates that performs a specific computation	Quantum algorithm design
Quantum Superposition	—	**Wave Property**	A qubit existing in multiple states simultaneously	Parallel processing of data
Quantum Entanglement	—	**Linked States**	Correlation between qubits, even at distance	Quantum communication and AI synchronization
Quantum Decoherence	—	**Loss of Quantum State**	When qubits lose their quantum behavior due to noise	Main limitation in today's systems
Quantum Error Correction	—	**Stability Control**	Protects information from decoherence	Reliable quantum computing
Quantum Measurement	—	**State Collapse**	Converts the probabilistic state into a definite outcome	Producing readable results

🌍 Analogy for Everyday Readers

If **bits** are like *flat paint colors*, each showing one tone at a time,
then **qubits** are *rainbows in motion* — blending all colors until you decide to look.
Only when measured (or "observed") does a qubit choose a single color — just as reality chooses one outcome from infinite possibilities.

💬 Quick Takeaway

The Qubit Family turns computing from logic into possibility — from "yes or no" to "maybe all at once."
This is the foundation for the coming age of **quantum artificial intelligence.**

⚡ The Watts Family

Definition and Overview

The **Watts Family** represents the energy backbone of the digital universe.
A **watt (W)** is a unit of power — the rate at which energy is consumed or converted. In computing, every process that runs, every bit that flips, and every prompt you submit consumes electrical energy measured in watts.

When multiple watts are measured over time, they become **watt-hours (Wh)**, **kilowatt-hours (kWh)**, or **megawatt-hours (MWh)** — the same units that appear on your electricity bill.
From powering your laptop to running massive AI data centers, the Watts Family governs the invisible current that brings artificial intelligence to life.

⚙️ Why Energy Matters to AI

AI doesn't just think — it *consumes*.
Every AI model requires energy for **training, storage, and inference** (the process of responding to prompts).
For example:

- Training a large model like GPT or Gemini can require energy equivalent to powering **hundreds of homes for a year**.
- Every prompt response you receive from an AI runs on GPUs (graphics processing units) that draw **hundreds to thousands of watts per second**.
- The world's biggest data centers, where these models live, are designed with energy optimization in mind — cooling, redundancy, and renewable energy integration.

Energy efficiency is now one of the **core frontiers of AI innovation.**
Companies and researchers aim to reduce carbon footprints through hardware design (like NVIDIA's energy-optimized GPUs), software efficiency (fewer parameters, better algorithms), and renewable power sourcing.

In essence, *energy is the heartbeat of intelligence.*
Without watts, even the smartest AI is silent.

🧠 Key Insight for Readers

Every prompt you send — every "conversation" with AI — triggers a real, physical reaction somewhere in the world.
Transistors switch, GPUs heat, fans spin, and electrons race through circuits.
That process costs energy, measured in watts, which converts electrical potential into computational intelligence.

The future of AI depends not just on smarter algorithms, but on **smarter energy management.**
Efficiency, sustainability, and innovation all begin with the Watts Family.

⚡ The Watts Family Tree

Member	Symbol / Abbreviation	Measurement	Explanation	Used In
Watt	`W`	1 Joule per second	The base unit of power	CPUs, GPUs, servers
Kilowatt	`kW`	1,000 Watts	Power scale for small systems	Desktops, local servers
Megawatt	`MW`	1,000 kW	Used for large data centers	AI data clusters
Gigawatt	`GW`	1,000 MW	City-level power output	Regional AI hubs
Watt-Hour	`Wh`	Power over time	Measures energy consumption	Battery usage
Kilowatt-Hour	`kWh`	1,000 Wh	Common billing unit	Energy tracking and optimization
Joule	`J`	1 Newton meter	Physical unit of energy	Thermodynamics, hardware physics
Calorie (small)	`cal`	4.184 Joules	Heat energy equivalent	Energy-to-heat conversion
Thermal Watt	—	—	Heat dissipated by hardware	Cooling and thermal systems
Efficiency Ratio	—	Output/Input (unitless)	Measures how much energy becomes useful work	AI energy optimization

🌍 Analogy for Everyday Readers

If information is *the brain* of AI, then **energy is its blood**.
Watts are what keep every digital neuron alive — from your phone's processor to the world's largest AI supercomputers.
No matter how intelligent a model becomes, without energy, it can't think, create, or respond.

💬 Quick Takeaway

The Watts Family fuels every AI breakthrough.
Intelligence without energy is potential; energy without control is waste.
The future belongs to technologies that learn to balance both.

What Is an LLM?

A **Large Language Model (LLM)** is an advanced type of artificial intelligence trained to understand, interpret, and generate human-style language.
Instead of memorizing facts, it learns by studying enormous collections of text—books, websites, articles, and digital conversations—to discover how words, ideas, and patterns connect.

At the heart of most LLMs is a **transformer architecture**, a deep neural network that processes many words at once and learns which ones influence each other. Through this structure, the model becomes capable of predicting the next word in a sentence, completing thoughts, or even creating entirely new text that sounds natural and context-aware.

What makes LLMs "large" is their **scale**—they contain billions or even trillions of parameters (the digital "neurons" that store learned knowledge). These parameters enable the model to perform countless language-based tasks, such as writing essays, generating computer code, summarizing information, answering questions, or translating text across languages.

However, an LLM doesn't truly *understand* meaning the way humans do. It predicts responses based on probability and patterns learned during training.
That's why your **prompts**—the instructions you give—are so important. The clearer and more intentional your wording, the more accurate, creative, and insightful the AI's replies will be.

This book will teach you how to communicate effectively with LLMs—to guide their reasoning, reduce errors, and unlock their full creative potential.

Human-Style Language

Definition:

Human-style language refers to the natural, expressive way people communicate — using tone, emotion, rhythm, and context that sound authentic to everyday conversation. When an AI model speaks or writes in "human style," it produces responses that feel **warm, relatable, and conversational**, rather than mechanical or robotic.

Key Characteristics

1. **Natural Flow:**
   Words and sentences follow the same rhythm and structure that people use when speaking or writing casually.
   Example:
   - Human-style: *"That's a great idea! Let's see how we can make it work."*
   - Robotic-style: *"Acknowledged. Idea is feasible. Proceeding to analyze."*
2. **Tone and Emotion:**
   It reflects mood — friendly, serious, professional, or empathetic — depending on the context of the conversation.
3. **Context Awareness:**
   The AI understands *how* something is said, not just *what* is said.
   It adjusts its wording based on the user's personality, topic, and goal.
4. **Personal Connection:**
   Uses pronouns ("you," "we," "I"), metaphors, and examples to sound more human and engaging.
5. **Adaptive Communication:**
   The AI can shift tone — casual, formal, educational, persuasive — just like a human speaker would in different situations.

Why It Matters in AI Communication

Human-style language helps bridge the gap between **technology and trust.**
When AI responds naturally, users feel understood, respected, and comfortable continuing the conversation.
It transforms AI from a tool into a **partner** — one that listens, empathizes, and communicates effectively.

In short:

"Human-style language makes AI sound like it's talking *with* you, not *at* you."

Example in AI Prompting

Prompt:

"Explain quantum computing in human-style language."

AI Response:

"Imagine a computer that doesn't just pick one answer at a time but explores many possibilities all at once — that's what quantum computing does."

✅ The explanation uses **everyday imagery**, **simple words**, and **a friendly tone** — hallmarks of human-style communication.

Applications

- **Customer Service Bots** that sound caring and helpful.
- **AI Tutors** that explain complex ideas in simple, human terms.
- **Writing Assistants** that produce conversational marketing or blog content.
- **AI Agents** (like the ones you're building for YourAIStudyBuddy.com) that teach or guide with empathy and clarity.

Summary

Human-style language is the art of making AI sound less like a computer and more like a companion.
It uses tone, empathy, and understanding to connect naturally with people.
In prompting, asking AI to "respond in human-style language" ensures the output feels authentic, easy to read, and emotionally intelligent.

Transformer Architecture

Definition:

The **Transformer architecture** is a deep learning model introduced in 2017 by Vaswani et al. in the paper *"Attention Is All You Need."*
It revolutionized artificial intelligence by enabling models to understand and generate human language more efficiently than ever before.
Transformers are now the backbone of large language models (LLMs) such as **ChatGPT, BERT, Gemini, Claude, and GPT-4.**

Key Concept: Attention Mechanism

At the heart of the Transformer is a system called **self-attention**, which allows the model to focus on the most important words in a sentence — regardless of their position.
Instead of reading text word-by-word like older models, Transformers process the entire sequence at once and learn **which words influence each other most strongly.**

Example:
In the sentence *"The cat sat on the mat because it was tired,"*

the Transformer knows that "it" refers to "the cat," not "the mat."
It learns this by assigning higher **attention weights** between related words.

Key Components

1. **Encoder:**
   - Reads and processes the input text.
   - Breaks the text into tokens and builds representations (embeddings).
   - Each encoder layer uses **self-attention** and **feed-forward networks** to understand relationships.
2. **Decoder:**
   - Generates output (for example, a translation or response).
   - Uses both **self-attention** (to understand its own generated words) and **cross-attention** (to relate them to the input).
3. **Positional Encoding:**
   - Since Transformers don't read sequentially like RNNs, positional encodings tell the model *where* each word appears in a sentence.
4. **Multi-Head Attention:**
   - The model uses several attention "heads" to look at relationships from multiple perspectives at once (syntax, meaning, emotion, etc.).
5. **Feed-Forward Layers:**
   - After attention, each layer passes data through small neural networks that refine and strengthen understanding.

Benefits

✅ **Parallel Processing:**
Processes all words at once instead of one at a time — much faster.

✅ **Better Context Understanding:**
Recognizes long-range dependencies between words in large texts.

✅ **Scalable:**
Can be trained on massive datasets for translation, summarization, question answering, and chatbots.

✅ **Transfer Learning:**
Pretrained models can be fine-tuned for new tasks with smaller datasets.

Disadvantages

⚠ **Resource Intensive:**
Requires huge amounts of memory and computing power.

⚠ **Black-Box Problem:**
Difficult to fully interpret how attention weights lead to specific outputs.

⚠ **Bias Retention:**
Can inherit biases from the training data.

Applications

- **Language Translation** (Google Translate)
- **Text Generation** (ChatGPT, Bard, Claude)
- **Summarization & Question Answering**
- **Speech Recognition and Image Captioning**
- **Code Generation** (GitHub Copilot, Replit Ghostwriter)

Analogy

A Transformer works like a team of readers highlighting a document.
Each reader focuses on different key words and phrases, then they combine their insights to produce a complete, context-aware understanding.

Summary

The **Transformer architecture** changed the field of AI forever.
It introduced a smarter, faster way for machines to understand human language using **attention** instead of repetition.
Because of this breakthrough, today's AI systems can write essays, translate speech, create art, and hold meaningful conversations.

🧠 Breaking Down the Transformer Architecture

Definition (In Simple Terms):

The **Transformer Architecture** is a framework that helps AI models understand and generate language.
It's built like a two-part machine — an **encoder** that reads information and a **decoder** that writes or predicts what comes next.
Its secret power comes from something called **"attention"** — the ability to focus on the most important parts of a sentence or context, just like how humans pay attention when listening or reading.

1. The Core Idea: "Attention Is All You Need"

Before Transformers, older models like RNNs (Recurrent Neural Networks) read text one word at a time, which was slow and hard for long sentences.
Transformers changed everything by allowing the model to **look at all words at once** and decide which ones matter most — this is called **self-attention**.

Example:
In the sentence:

"The cat sat on the mat because it was tired."
The Transformer learns that **"it"** refers to **"the cat,"** not the mat.
It "pays attention" to the right relationship automatically.

2. The Two Main Parts

A. Encoder – The Reader

The **encoder** takes in the input text (your question, sentence, or paragraph) and converts it into numbers the AI can understand (called **embeddings**).

Each encoder layer performs two main jobs:

1. **Self-Attention:** Finds relationships between words.
2. **Feed-Forward Layer:** Refines those relationships mathematically to build meaning.

Encoders are stacked — often 6 to 12 layers deep — to build rich understanding.

B. Decoder – The Writer

The **decoder** uses what the encoder learned and generates an output — word by word — predicting what comes next.

Each decoder layer also performs two jobs:

1. **Self-Attention (on the output so far):** Understands what it has already generated.
2. **Cross-Attention:** Connects its generated text back to the encoded input for accuracy.

That's how AI can take a prompt like:

"Write a story about a robot learning kindness,"
and output a complete story that stays on topic and emotionally consistent.

3. How the Transformer Works — Step by Step

Here's the process in simple stages:

Step	What Happens	Example in Human Terms
1 Input	Text is split into tokens (words/pieces).	Like breaking a sentence into puzzle pieces.

Step	What Happens	Example in Human Terms
2 Embedding	Tokens are converted into vectors (numbers).	Giving each word its "meaning code."
3 Positional Encoding	Adds information about word order.	Knowing "dog bites man" ≠ "man bites dog."
4 Attention	Model finds relationships between words.	Decides which words relate most strongly.
5 Feed-Forward	Data passes through small neural layers.	Refines understanding of meaning.
6 Output	Decoder predicts next words or sentences.	Writes, translates, or answers clearly.

4. Key Components (In Simple Language)

Component	Purpose	Analogy
Self-Attention	Helps AI focus on important words in context.	Like highlighting key ideas in a paragraph.
Multi-Head Attention	Looks at multiple meanings or patterns at once.	Like several readers focusing on different parts of the same story.
Positional Encoding	Reminds the AI of word order.	Like giving each word its address in a sentence.
Feed-Forward Network	Adds depth and refinement.	Like summarizing what you learned from reading.
Normalization	Keeps data balanced and stable.	Like editing your thoughts before speaking.
Softmax Layer	Chooses the most likely next word.	Like picking the best answer out of many options.

5. Why Transformers Changed Everything

✅ **Speed:**
They process all words simultaneously, not one by one.

✅ **Context Understanding:**
They remember long-range relationships (for example, "he" in paragraph three referring to "John" in paragraph one).

✅ **Scalability:**
They can grow in size (GPT-3, GPT-4, Claude, etc.) without losing performance.

✅ **Adaptability:**
They can handle text, images, audio, and even video — all using similar architecture.

6. Real-World Examples

AI Model	Built On Transformer?	Purpose
BERT (Google)	✅ Yes	Understanding sentence meaning for search.
GPT Series (OpenAI)	✅ Yes	Generating human-like text and conversations.
T5 (Google)	✅ Yes	Translating, summarizing, and text rewriting.
Vision Transformers (ViT)	✅ Yes	Understanding images like a human brain.

7. Summary (In Human Style)

The **Transformer Architecture** is like a powerful translator between human language and machine understanding.
It reads everything at once, pays attention to what matters, and learns relationships that give meaning to text.

Because of Transformers, AI can now:

- Write books.
- Translate languages.
- Create music.
- Understand emotion and context.

It's the reason why when you talk to AI today — it sounds natural, intelligent, and human-like.

Diagram: How the Transformer Architecture Works

```
TRANSFORMER ARCHITECTURE

        ▲
        |

      INPUT
 (Text or Tokens)

        |
        ▼

  EMBEDDING LAYER
Converts words into vectors
```

POSITIONAL ENCODING
Adds word order information

↓

ENCODER
(Reads and understands input)

1 SELF-ATTENTION: Focuses on relationships between all words in a sentence.
Example: Knows "it" refers to "the cat."

2 FEED-FORWARD NETWORK: Refines and strengthens contextual understanding.

(These encoder layers stack 6–12 times for deep learning.)

↓

DECODER
(Generates and predicts output)

1 SELF-ATTENTION: Looks at what it's already written.
Helps keep sentences consistent.

2 CROSS-ATTENTION: Connects decoder to encoder data.
Ensures the response matches the input's meaning.

3 FEED-FORWARD LAYERS: Final refinement and output.

↓

OUTPUT
(Predicted words, text, etc.)

🧩 Simple Flow Summary

Step	What Happens	Purpose
1	Input text is broken into tokens.	Prepares words for processing.
2	Embeddings + positional encoding applied.	Adds meaning and order.
3	Encoder analyzes and builds understanding.	Learns context and relationships.
4	Decoder generates new words step by step.	Produces sentences or translations.
5	Output becomes the final human-style text.	You see the answer or completion.

💡 Quick Analogy

The Transformer works like a skilled translator team:
One side (Encoder) *reads and understands everything*,
the other side (Decoder) *writes and speaks fluently* —
and both communicate through attention to make sure every idea stays connected.

Figure 11.2 – How the Attention Mechanism Works in a Transformer

Diagram: The Attention Mechanism Explained

```
ATTENTION MECHANISM (Simplified)
        ▲
        |
Input Sentence
"The cat sat on the mat
 because it was tired."
        |
        ▼
Step 1: Tokenization
Each word is split and given an ID.
[The] [cat] [sat] [on] [the] [mat] [because]
[it] [was] [tired]
        |
        ▼
Step 2: Embedding
Words are converted into numeric vectors
(representing meaning, not just spelling).
        |
        ▼
Step 3: Self-Attention
The model looks at ALL words at once
and decides which ones are related.
        |
        ▼
Example Focus:
When analyzing the word "it," the AI
gives highest attention weight to "cat" —
because "it" refers to "the cat."
        |
        ▼
Step 4: Attention Weights
Numbers (0.0 to 1.0) show connection strength
Example:
 "it" → "cat" = 0.95 (strong link)
 "it" → "mat" = 0.15 (weak link)
        |
        ▼
Step 5: Weighted Context
Each word is re-represented with weighted
meanings — forming a rich understanding
of the entire sentence.
        |
        ▼
Step 6: Output
The AI now "understands" the relationships
and can predict or generate accurate text.
```

🧩 In Simple Words

Attention is how AI learns to *focus* — it doesn't treat every word equally.
Instead, it gives **more weight** to the words that matter most for meaning.

💡 Analogy

Think of attention like reading comprehension:
When you read a sentence, your brain automatically highlights the important words that give context to the rest.
The Transformer does the same — it *pays attention* to what's relevant and ignores what's not.

📊 Key Benefit

This mechanism allows the AI to:

- Understand long sentences easily.
- Keep context even in large paragraphs.
- Translate meaning across languages.
- Sound more *human-style* and context-aware in its replies.

Top 10 LLMs (2025) — Notable Models to Know

Below is a snapshot of some of the most influential and capable LLMs today. Use this as a reference in your prompt experiments and comparative thinking.

#	Model	Highlights / Use Cases
1	**GPT-4.5 / GPT Series (OpenAI)**	The flagship series behind ChatGPT, strong in reasoning, writing, and tool integration.
2	**Claude (Anthropic)**	Known for alignment and safe responses, with versions like Claude 3.7 and Claude 4.
3	**Gemini (Google)**	Multimodal (text, image, audio), long-context capability, integrated into Google services. Zapier+1
4	**LLaMA (Meta)**	Meta's open / community-friendly family of models; increasingly powerful in each release. Instaclustr+2TechTarget+2
5	**Mistral**	Strong open-source contender, good balance between performance and resource cost. Klu+1
6	**DeepSeek-V3**	Emerging model with high capability in math, code, and reasoning. Splunk+2Codingscape+2
7	**Falcon**	Open model strong in speed and efficiency, used for many real-world applications. TechTarget+1
8	**Grok (xAI)**	Launched by Elon Musk's xAI; designed for conversational and reasoning tasks.
9	**Qwen (Alibaba / Open Source)**	Good multilingual and instruction-tuned model; strong in code and reasoning. KDnuggets+1
10	**Nemotron / Other Experimental / Future Models**	Cutting-edge architectures often in research or limited release, worth watching as the field develops.

Note: This list is illustrative and may evolve as new models appear or existing ones improve. Always test with your own prompts and goals.

🔠 The Token Family

Definition and Overview

The **Token Family** represents the language currency of artificial intelligence — the smallest readable unit of meaning that an AI model understands.
Just as humans read words and sentences, large language models (LLMs) process **tokens**.
A *token* can be a single letter, a word, or even part of a word, depending on the language model's design. For example:

- "Apple" might count as **one token**.
- "Artificial intelligence" might count as **three tokens** — "Artificial," "intelli," and "gence."

Tokens are how AI breaks your text into manageable pieces for understanding, prediction, and response generation.
They are to language models what **bits and bytes** are to computers — the fundamental building blocks of communication.

⚙️ Why Tokens Matter in Prompt Engineering

Every prompt you send to an AI is converted into tokens before the model begins to "think."
When you type a sentence, the system doesn't see words; it sees **token sequences** arranged in specific patterns.
Each token has meaning, probability, and position within a context window — and this determines how the model interprets your intent.

- **Clarity of your prompt** depends on token selection.
- **Cost and efficiency** of AI use depend on token count (most platforms charge per token).
- **Accuracy of responses** depends on how tokens connect logically in context.

Prompt engineers who understand tokens can control how much information to include, how to shape the tone, and how to avoid "token overflow" errors that cut off responses.

🧠 Key Insight for Readers

Think of tokens as **the vocabulary of AI thought**.
Every idea you express to a language model is translated into tokens, and every idea the AI returns is built from them.
Learning to "think in tokens" helps you write sharper prompts, manage limits, and predict how an AI will respond.

The Token Family Tree

Member	Definition	Typical Size / Meaning	Used For
Token	The smallest unit of meaning recognized by an AI model	Can be a single character, word, or part of a word	Understanding and generating text
Sub-Token	A fragment of a larger word	For example, "computa" + "tion" = "computation"	Language segmentation in AI
Context Window	The total number of tokens an AI model can "remember" at once	GPT-4: ~128K tokens; Gemini 2.0: up to 1M tokens	Maintaining conversation history and coherence
Input Tokens	Tokens you send to the model	Each character, space, or punctuation mark contributes	Determines cost and complexity of a prompt
Output Tokens	Tokens generated by the model	The response size in text form	Affects completeness and quality of answers
Token Limit	The model's maximum token capacity	Once exceeded, the earliest tokens are forgotten	Memory management in long conversations
Tokenization	The process of breaking text into tokens	Example: "I love AI." → ["I", "love", "AI", "."]	Model's preprocessing step
Embeddings	Numeric representation of tokens in multidimensional space	Used to measure similarity between ideas or words	Semantic search and AI reasoning
Token Probability	Likelihood of each token following the last one	Governs how the model predicts the next word	Core to AI text generation
Compression Token	Tokens that summarize or condense long input	Used in memory-efficient models	Long context compression and summarization

Analogy for Everyday Readers

If language is a song, **tokens are the notes**.
AI doesn't hear your sentences all at once — it plays them note by note, predicting what should come next based on the tune you're creating with your prompt.

💬 Quick Takeaway

Tokens are the heartbeat of every conversation with AI.
The better you understand how they flow, the more fluent you become in speaking the language of machines.

🧩 The Parameter Family

Definition and Overview

The **Parameter Family** represents the *memory and intelligence* of artificial intelligence models.
Parameters are the adjustable values — or "weights" — inside a neural network that determine how an AI processes information, makes predictions, and learns patterns.

Each parameter acts like a **tiny decision-maker**.
When combined, millions or billions of parameters form complex systems capable of language understanding, image recognition, and reasoning.
For example:

- A small model might have **100 million parameters**.
- A large model like GPT-4 or Gemini may have **over a trillion parameters**.

In simple terms:

Tokens are the words AI reads.
Parameters are how AI remembers what those words mean.

Why Parameters Matter in AI and Prompt Engineering

Parameters determine the *quality, accuracy, and style* of an AI's response.
They are what make one model creative and another factual, one brief and another verbose.
When you send a prompt, your text activates specific networks of parameters that were adjusted during training — this is how the model "knows" how to reply.

Key impacts of parameters:

- **Precision:** More parameters can improve nuance, logic, and accuracy.
- **Creativity:** Well-tuned parameters allow models to generate new, coherent ideas.
- **Control:** Fine-tuned models (custom-trained) adjust parameters for specific industries, tones, or audiences.

Prompt engineers often "work around" parameters — not by changing them directly, but by learning to *influence* them through better instructions, role cues, and structure.

🧠 Key Insight for Readers

Think of parameters as the **neurons of artificial intelligence**.
Each one contributes a tiny piece of knowledge.
Together, they shape the model's personality, expertise, and logic.

Every time you prompt an AI effectively, you are *activating the right cluster of parameters* to produce a meaningful answer.

🧮 The Parameter Family Tree

Member	Definition	Scale / Size	Used For
Parameter	A numeric value (weight) adjusted during training	Ranges from thousands to trillions	Defines how input data is interpreted
Weight	The strength of a connection between two neurons	Controls how signals travel through layers	Model learning and prediction
Bias	A constant value added to help the model adjust	Prevents uniform outputs	Balancing outputs for realism
Layer	A collection of parameters working together	Input, hidden, and output layers	Processing information at different stages
Node / Neuron	A computational unit holding parameter values	The "cells" of a neural network	Information transfer and activation
Activation Function	Formula that decides if a neuron activates	e.g., ReLU, Sigmoid, Softmax	Adds non-linear decision power
Gradient	Rate of change in parameters during training	Guides updates through backpropagation	Learning efficiency
Training Epoch	A full cycle through the dataset	Adjusts parameters incrementally	Model learning iteration
Fine-Tuned Parameter	Adjusted after initial training	Specialization for niche tasks	Industry or domain customization
Frozen Parameter	Locked value not updated during training	Reduces overfitting, speeds up learning	Transfer learning models

🌍 Analogy for Everyday Readers

If tokens are the *words* of AI, parameters are the *understanding behind those words*. Each parameter is like a muscle fiber — on its own, small and simple, but when billions move in harmony, they create intelligence.

⚡ How Parameters Connect to Energy (Watts Family)

Every parameter consumes energy to store, update, and compute.
The more parameters a model has, the greater its **energy footprint** during training and inference.
This is why researchers focus on **parameter-efficient tuning (PET)** — making AI smarter without increasing energy use.

💬 Quick Takeaway

Parameters are the memories and instincts of AI.
They hold what the model has learned, guiding every response, every decision, and every word that follows.

🧠 The Neural Network Family

Definition and Overview

The **Neural Network Family** forms the structural foundation of modern artificial intelligence.
Inspired by the human brain, a neural network is made up of layers of interconnected nodes (or "neurons") that process information, recognize patterns, and make predictions.

Each neuron in a network receives input, performs a simple calculation, and passes the result to the next layer. When millions or billions of these neurons work together, they can learn to identify faces, understand language, compose music, or even carry on a conversation.

In short:

Neural networks are **how AI thinks.**
Parameters are **what AI remembers.**
Tokens are **what AI reads and writes.**

This family powers everything from chatbots and recommendation engines to self-driving cars and medical image analysis.

⚙️ Why Neural Networks Matter in AI and Prompt Engineering

When you type a prompt, your words are converted into tokens and sent through the model's **neural architecture**.
Each layer of this network interprets the text at a different level:

- Some layers detect grammar and word order.
- Others extract meaning and emotional tone.

- The deepest layers connect everything to context and reasoning.

The **structure** of a neural network determines how intelligently and efficiently a model responds to prompts.
A prompt engineer who understands this process can design instructions that align better with how neural networks process language — resulting in clearer, more logical, and more creative outputs.

🧩 Key Insight for Readers

Neural networks don't "think" like humans — but they *learn* through exposure and repetition.
Just as people improve through practice, networks improve through **training**, gradually adjusting their internal parameters until they can predict accurate outcomes.

When you communicate with AI, you're not just talking to a machine; you're interacting with a digital brain built on mathematical neurons and connections.

🧬 The Neural Network Family Tree

Member	Definition	Purpose	Example / Application
Neuron (Node)	Basic unit of computation that processes input data	Performs calculations and passes results forward	Like brain cells for AI
Layer	A group of neurons working together	Extracts patterns or features from input	Input, hidden, and output layers
Feedforward Network	Data moves in one direction only	Simplest type of neural network	Basic prediction tasks
Recurrent Neural Network (RNN)	Loops information through time	Handles sequences like text and speech	Language modeling, time-series analysis
Convolutional Neural Network (CNN)	Uses filters to process spatial data	Detects edges, shapes, and patterns	Image recognition, computer vision
Transformer Network	Uses self-attention to process all tokens at once	Foundation of modern LLMs	GPT, Gemini, Claude, Mistral
Activation Function	Determines if a neuron "fires" or stays inactive	Adds non-linearity for complex decision-making	ReLU, Sigmoid, Softmax
Loss Function	Measures error between prediction and truth	Guides model training	Mean Squared Error, Cross Entropy

Member	Definition	Purpose	Example / Application
Backpropagation	Algorithm that adjusts parameters to reduce error	Core of machine learning	Used in every deep learning model
Attention Mechanism	Focuses on important parts of the input sequence	Improves context understanding	Critical in transformers and chatbots

🌍 Analogy for Everyday Readers

If an AI model were a human brain:

- **Neurons** are individual brain cells.
- **Layers** are brain regions that specialize in different tasks.
- **Connections (parameters)** are synapses that strengthen with learning.

When you prompt AI, your words travel through this digital brain — activating pathways that have learned how to reason, write, and respond.

⚡ The Role of Energy (Watts Family)

Every neural network operation — from one neuron firing to a million-layer transformer running — consumes energy.
Training a deep network can require **megawatts of power**, while efficient inference depends on chip design and model optimization.
Balancing performance with energy efficiency is a major engineering challenge in modern AI.

💬 Quick Takeaway

The Neural Network Family is the mind of AI.
It connects memory (parameters), language (tokens), and power (watts) into one intelligent system capable of learning from data and responding to you in real time.

💡 What Is a "Chip Family"?

In computing and electronics, a **chip** (or microchip / integrated circuit) is a small electronic device made from semiconductor material that contains many transistors, resistors, and other components. A **chip family** refers to a series of related chips sharing core architecture, design principles, or functional roles. For example, a chip family might include variants for higher performance, more memory, lower power use, or specialized features.

Chip families are important because:

- They simplify design reuse. Engineers can build for one architecture and scale up/down.
- They offer predictable upgrades. You can move within a family without redesigning entirely.
- They allow specialization (e.g. general CPU, graphics, AI accelerator, DSP) under a common interface.

In the world of prompt engineering and AI, knowing about chips matters because AI models run on **accelerators** (GPUs, TPUs, NPUs), which are specialized chips optimized for parallel computation — matrix math, tensor operations, etc. The choice of chip family affects model speed, power, cost, and capabilities.

🗂 The Dataset Family

Definition and Overview

The **Dataset Family** represents the *knowledge and experience* of artificial intelligence.
A **dataset** is a structured collection of information used to train, test, and evaluate AI models. It is the digital equivalent of memory, textbooks, and life experience combined.

Datasets teach machines how to recognize patterns, translate languages, generate images, and respond intelligently to prompts.
Without data, no neural network — no matter how powerful — could ever learn.

In short:

The Dataset Family is to AI what experience is to humans — the source of all learning, reasoning, and understanding.

AI models like GPT, Gemini, and Claude learn from vast collections of text, images, code, and audio. These collections form their worldviews — shaping how they interpret your prompts and generate answers.

⚙ Why Datasets Matter in AI and Prompt Engineering

Every AI's response is based on the information it was trained on.
When you prompt an AI, it doesn't access the internet directly (unless connected in real time); it draws from patterns it learned during training.

That means the **quality of a model's dataset** determines the quality of its responses.

- **High-quality, diverse data** = accurate, balanced, and creative outputs.
- **Poor or biased data** = limited, repetitive, or misleading results.

For prompt engineers, understanding datasets helps explain why certain models excel at technical writing while others perform better at storytelling.

It also helps users craft prompts that align with a model's strengths — or compensate for its blind spots.

🧠 Key Insight for Readers

AI doesn't "know" facts — it recognizes *patterns of language and logic* learned from data.
Datasets are not just information; they are **imprints of human knowledge** encoded in digital form.
Every bias, truth, innovation, and error in our world is reflected in them.

When you understand how datasets shape AI's behavior, you learn how to *guide* that behavior through careful prompting.

🗄 The Dataset Family Tree

Member	Definition	Example	Used For
Dataset	A structured collection of data used for training	Wikipedia text, image libraries, or speech recordings	Teaching AI concepts and patterns
Training Dataset	The main data the model learns from	Massive text or image archives	Learning relationships and patterns
Validation Dataset	Data used to test accuracy during training	Separate from training data	Preventing overfitting and bias
Test Dataset	Final evaluation data	New examples never seen before	Measuring model performance
Labeled Dataset	Data with predefined tags or answers	Image labeled "dog" or "cat"	Supervised learning
Unlabeled Dataset	Data without categories or answers	Raw text, photos, or videos	Unsupervised or self-learning AI
Synthetic Dataset	Artificially generated data	AI-generated images or sentences	Expanding limited datasets safely
Multimodal Dataset	Contains more than one data type	Text, images, and sound together	Training multimodal AIs like Gemini
Balanced Dataset	Equal representation of categories	Equal gender or region samples	Reducing bias and improving fairness
Open Dataset	Freely available for research	COCO, ImageNet, Common Crawl	Publicly accessible training data

🌍 Analogy for Everyday Readers

If a **neural network** is the brain,
and **parameters** are the neurons,
then the **Dataset Family** is the *world the AI grew up in.*

Just like people are shaped by their experiences, AI is shaped by its data.
If it learns from biased, incomplete, or repetitive sources, its "personality" and accuracy will reflect that.

⚡ The Energy Connection (Watts Family)

Datasets also consume massive amounts of energy during training.
Feeding billions of data samples through neural networks requires weeks or even months of continuous computation in high-powered data centers.
This is why sustainable computing — optimizing energy per dataset processed — is now a critical field of AI research.

💬 Quick Takeaway

The Dataset Family is the memory of humanity, digitized for machines.
Its quality defines how well AI understands us — and how accurately it speaks back.

🤖 The AI Agent Family

Definition and Overview

The **AI Agent Family** represents the *action-oriented generation* of artificial intelligence — systems designed not just to think, but to **act**.
An **AI agent** is a program capable of perceiving its environment, processing information, making decisions, and performing tasks autonomously or semi-autonomously.

In simple terms:

While a traditional AI model responds to a question, an AI agent **takes initiative** to achieve a goal.

These agents combine multiple "families" of AI:

- **Datasets** give them knowledge.

- **Neural networks** give them reasoning.
- **Tokens and parameters** give them language.
- **Energy and chips** give them power.
  Together, they form a dynamic ecosystem of intelligence that can plan, learn, and adapt.

⚙️ Why AI Agents Matter in Prompt Engineering

AI agents are at the heart of *applied prompt engineering*.
Instead of writing one prompt at a time, prompt engineers now design **multi-step instructions, goal hierarchies, and chain-of-thought frameworks** that guide agents to complete full workflows.

For example:

- A **Customer Support Agent** can answer user questions, escalate issues, and summarize chat logs.
- A **Research Agent** can gather information, analyze it, and produce summaries or reports.
- A **Marketing Agent** can brainstorm ideas, write posts, and even schedule content.

Every agent begins with a **core prompt** — a set of rules and goals that define its behavior.
That prompt acts like its *personality and purpose,* shaping how it responds, prioritizes, and learns.

🧠 Key Insight for Readers

AI agents represent the **bridge between human intention and machine execution.**
Where prompt engineering focuses on *communication,* agent design focuses on *collaboration.*
Agents are built to think, remember, and act — often working with other agents in teams.

This means prompt engineers are not just writers — they're **AI architects**, designing workflows that mimic human teamwork.

🧩 The AI Agent Family Tree

Member	Definition	Core Function	Example Use
Reactive Agent	Responds to immediate inputs	Acts without long-term memory	Chatbots, voice assistants
Deliberative Agent	Plans actions based on reasoning	Uses internal models to make decisions	Research or planning bots
Learning Agent	Improves performance over time	Adapts behavior from feedback	Recommendation systems

Member	Definition	Core Function	Example Use
Collaborative Agent	Works with humans or other agents	Shares information and tasks	Customer service teams
Autonomous Agent	Operates independently	Executes actions without constant supervision	Automated scheduling bots
Goal-Based Agent	Follows specific objectives	Tracks and measures progress	Sales forecasting or project planning
Rule-Based Agent	Acts based on predefined logic	Simple if-then decisions	Security or compliance checks
Multi-Agent System	Group of agents working together	Distributes tasks across models	AI ecosystems or workflow networks
Embodied Agent	Exists in physical or virtual form	Interacts through motion or simulation	Robots, VR companions
Cognitive Agent	Simulates human-like thinking	Uses reasoning, memory, and adaptation	AI tutors, creative writing assistants

🌍 Analogy for Everyday Readers

If AI models are **students**, then AI agents are **graduates** — ready to enter the real world and apply what they've learned.
They don't just answer; they *act*.
They can schedule your meetings, analyze data, generate content, or even collaborate with other AI systems — all starting from the power of a well-engineered prompt.

⚡ The Energy and Hardware Connection

Every AI agent runs on energy (Watts Family) and hardware (Chip Family).
The more complex the agent's reasoning and task execution, the greater its energy and computational demand.
This is why optimizing prompts — giving clear, structured instructions — not only improves accuracy but also **saves energy and processing time.**

💬 Quick Takeaway

The AI Agent Family transforms intelligence into action.
They are the doers of the AI world — autonomous collaborators who bring prompts, parameters, and data to life.

💬 The Prompt Family

Definition and Overview

The **Prompt Family** represents the *language of communication* between humans and artificial intelligence.
A **prompt** is any instruction, question, or input that guides an AI system toward a desired output.
In essence, it's how we *talk* to AI — and how AI learns to *talk back.*

Every AI model, from simple chatbots to massive large language models (LLMs), relies on prompts to generate meaning.
A prompt can be a few words ("Write a poem about friendship") or a detailed directive with structure, role, tone, and context.

In short:

The Prompt Family is the *voice of intelligence* — the art and science of communicating with machines in human terms.

⚙️ Why the Prompt Family Matters

Prompts are not just inputs — they are **blueprints** for behavior.
The way you phrase a prompt directly affects what the AI understands, how it reasons, and the quality of its response.

Every profession, from education to law to marketing, can be transformed by mastering prompt communication.
Prompt engineering gives humans the power to:

- Direct AI creativity toward specific outcomes.
- Control the tone, accuracy, and structure of responses.
- Build multi-step workflows and automated agents that act intelligently.

The better the prompt, the smarter the AI seems.

🧠 Key Insight for Readers

Every AI model is a mirror reflecting your clarity, intent, and creativity.
If the input is vague, the output will be generic.
If the input is structured, specific, and contextual, the AI will respond with precision and intelligence.

This is why prompt engineering has become the **new literacy of the AI era.**
It's not coding — it's communication.
The Prompt Family transforms words into logic, logic into action, and action into results.

🧬 The Prompt Family Tree

Member	Definition	Purpose	Example
Prompt	A command or instruction that directs AI output	Initiates the AI's thinking process	"Write a 3-paragraph essay on renewable energy."
System Prompt	The foundational directive that defines how an AI behaves	Sets tone, rules, and personality	"You are a helpful assistant that writes in a formal tone."
User Prompt	Input provided by the user	Requests specific output	"Summarize this article in 100 words."
Chain Prompt	Multi-step instruction linking tasks together	Breaks complex tasks into stages	"First outline, then write, then edit the paragraph."
Few-Shot Prompt	Provides examples to teach a pattern	Guides AI through imitation	"Translate: Hello=Hola, Goodbye=Adiós, Thank you=?"
Zero-Shot Prompt	No examples given — AI relies on general training	Used for flexible tasks	"Generate 5 creative slogans for a bakery."
Role Prompt	Assigns a personality or expertise to the AI	Shapes behavior and tone	"Act as a marketing expert."
Context Prompt	Adds background, goals, or purpose	Improves relevance	"Write for a middle school audience."
Constraint Prompt	Sets boundaries like tone, format, or length	Ensures precision	"Write 3 sentences, no more than 50 words each."
Recursive Prompt	Feeds outputs back into inputs for refinement	Enables self-improvement	"Revise your previous answer for more clarity."

🌑 Analogy for Everyday Readers

Think of a **prompt** as a *conversation starter* between human intention and machine intelligence.
Just like a teacher gives an assignment, a director gives a script, or a coach gives strategy — the AI follows your instruction with its own interpretation of what success means.

You are not commanding a machine; you're **collaborating with a digital thinker.**

⚡ The Prompt-to-Power Connection

Prompts may look small, but each one activates millions (sometimes billions) of computations across neural layers.
A well-written prompt can save both **energy (Watts Family)** and **processing time (Chip Family)** because it helps the model reach the right output faster — without wasted computation.
This is why clear prompting isn't just smart; it's **efficient engineering.**

💡 The 4 C's in the Prompt Family

Your book beautifully introduces the **4 C's Framework** of effective prompting — **Clarity, Context, Constraints, and Creativity.**
Each C represents a discipline within the Prompt Family:

- **Clarity** ensures your meaning is unmistakable.
- **Context** gives direction and purpose.
- **Constraints** create focus and discipline.
- **Creativity** brings life, variety, and originality.

Together, they transform raw AI power into usable human intelligence.

💬 Quick Takeaway

The Prompt Family is the bridge between human intelligence and artificial intelligence.
It's how we translate intention into instruction — and imagination into innovation.

🧠 The Memory Family

Definition and Overview

The **Memory Family** represents the *cognitive backbone* of artificial intelligence — the part that allows AI systems to remember context, store information, and build continuity across interactions.

In traditional computing, memory is simply storage — a place to keep data.
But in AI, memory goes beyond storage. It allows models to *retain context* from previous inputs, *reference earlier data,* and *maintain coherent conversations* over time.

In short:

The Memory Family is the reason AI can remember what you said, understand what you mean, and build upon it intelligently.

⚙️ Why the Memory Family Matters

When you talk to an AI, you are not just giving it instructions — you are building a **relationship of context**.
Every prompt, response, and clarification becomes part of an evolving conversation that the AI interprets dynamically.

This memory-driven design allows for:

- **Personalization** — AI adapts to your style, goals, and preferences.
- **Continuity** — You can build long-form projects or conversations without repeating instructions.
- **Contextual Awareness** — The AI understands references like "that idea" or "the previous answer."

For prompt engineers, understanding memory means learning how to use context effectively — when to remind, reset, or refine the AI's internal state for optimal results.

🧩 The Memory Family Tree

Member	Definition	Function	Example Use
Short-Term Memory	Temporary context used during a single session	Holds information briefly for continuity	AI remembering the last few messages
Long-Term Memory	Persistent memory that stores facts, preferences, or history	Retains data across sessions	AI remembering your project or writing style
Working Memory	Active mental space where current thoughts are processed	Allows reasoning and context-switching	Comparing two previous ideas in real-time
Episodic Memory	Memory of past interactions or experiences	Helps AI "recall" specific conversations	"You asked me this yesterday, and here's what we found."
Semantic Memory	Stored knowledge about the world	Powers general reasoning and common sense	Knowing that Paris is the capital of France
Vector Memory	Mathematical embedding of meaning	Enables retrieval of semantically related ideas	Finding similar words or related concepts
External Memory	Linked to external tools or databases	Extends AI's recall and learning power	Notion, Google Drive, or API-connected memory

Member	Definition	Function	Example Use
Context Window	The limited number of tokens AI can "see" at one time	Determines how much the AI can remember per session	Models like GPT-4 can handle 128k tokens
Selective Memory	Filters what is important to retain or forget	Keeps relevant details, discards noise	Prioritizing user goals over small talk
Memory Bank	Combined system for long-term learning	Central hub for multi-agent recall	Used in multi-agent and adaptive systems

🌍 Analogy for Everyday Readers

Think of AI's memory like a human conversation:

- **Short-term memory** is remembering what was just said.
- **Long-term memory** is remembering your friend's birthday.
- **Working memory** is juggling ideas mid-discussion.
- **Episodic memory** is recalling last week's lunch conversation.

AI functions the same way — except its memory is built from data structures, embeddings, and context tokens instead of neurons and synapses.

⚡ How Memory Powers Prompt Engineering

Prompt engineering depends heavily on *context retention.*
Without memory, each prompt is isolated — like talking to someone who forgets everything after every sentence.

By designing prompts that reference earlier ideas ("As mentioned before…" or "Using the previous summary…"), you leverage AI's short-term and working memory to build deeper, smarter responses.
In systems with long-term memory, you can train the AI to *grow* — remembering your projects, tone, and goals over time.

🔋 Energy and Efficiency Connection

Every time an AI retrieves or processes memory, it consumes computational power (Watts Family) and activates neural parameters (Parameter Family).
This is why managing memory efficiently — avoiding unnecessary repetition — helps optimize both **energy use and response quality.**

💬 Quick Takeaway

The Memory Family allows AI to think in context, respond intelligently, and build lasting connections with users.
Without it, AI would be brilliant — but forgetful.

🧩 The Knowledge Family

Definition and Overview

The **Knowledge Family** represents the *intellectual core* of artificial intelligence — the systems, datasets, and mechanisms that enable AI to "know," "understand," and "reason" about the world.

In humans, knowledge comes from experience and learning.
In AI, knowledge comes from **data, models, and relationships between information.** It's how the machine connects words to meanings, patterns to predictions, and questions to coherent answers.

In simple terms:

The Knowledge Family is the *brain of AI's intelligence* — the part that transforms data into understanding and understanding into insight.

⚙️ Why the Knowledge Family Matters

Knowledge is what makes AI useful, reliable, and insightful.
Without knowledge, an AI model is just a blank slate — capable of computation but empty of meaning.

AI's knowledge base defines:

- How accurately it answers factual questions.
- How well it reasons about real-world topics.
- How deeply it understands concepts, logic, and relationships.

Prompt engineers rely on knowledge awareness to craft more effective prompts — knowing *what* a model likely knows, *what* it doesn't, and *how* to guide it toward more informed responses.

🧠 How AI Builds Knowledge

AI does not "know" facts the way humans do.
Instead, it **represents** knowledge mathematically through *weights, embeddings, and patterns* in neural networks.

When AI is trained, it processes billions of examples, adjusting its internal connections until it can predict what comes next — whether a word, a phrase, or a solution.
Over time, these patterns form a web of meaning that acts as its internal knowledge base.

That's why AI can answer:

- "What is the capital of Japan?"
- "Why does the sun rise in the east?"
- "How do neural networks learn?"

It's not recalling facts — it's reproducing learned patterns of reasoning.

🧬 The Knowledge Family Tree

Member	Definition	Purpose	Example Use
Knowledge Base	A structured collection of facts and information	Stores factual or logical data	Wikipedia, Wikidata, or private enterprise databases
Knowledge Graph	A network of connected data points showing relationships	Helps AI understand context and meaning	Google Knowledge Graph
Embedded Knowledge	Information encoded within AI model parameters	Powers large language models	GPT and Claude's internal reasoning
Explicit Knowledge	Clearly defined and structured data	Easy to read and retrieve	Rules, formulas, or FAQs
Tacit Knowledge	Implicit understanding learned through patterns	Hard to define but powerful for predictions	Style imitation or natural conversation
Procedural Knowledge	"Know-how" knowledge for completing tasks	Guides actions or processes	Step-by-step instructions or skill tasks
Declarative Knowledge	"Know-that" knowledge about facts or information	Used for factual Q&A or summaries	"Paris is the capital of France."
Domain Knowledge	Specialized understanding in a specific field	Provides expertise in niche areas	Medical, legal, or engineering data
Knowledge Distillation	The process of transferring knowledge from one model to another	Optimizes smaller, faster models	Compressing GPT-4 into smaller AI assistants
Retrieval-Augmented Knowledge	Dynamic knowledge pulled from external sources	Expands AI's real-time understanding	AI connected to the web or databases

🌍 Analogy for Everyday Readers

Think of **The Knowledge Family** as a vast **library inside the AI's brain.**

- **Memory** helps AI remember *where* the books are.
- **Knowledge** helps AI *understand what's inside* them.

When you talk to AI, you're not just asking for data — you're inviting it to reason, compare, and synthesize insights across everything it has ever learned.

⚡ Knowledge and the Prompt Connection

Prompt engineering becomes far more effective when you know how to tap into AI's knowledge base.
For example:

- Instead of asking *"What is AI?"*, ask *"Explain AI to a beginner using simple analogies."*
  That prompt engages **declarative knowledge** (facts) and **tacit knowledge** (communication style).

You're not just accessing data — you're unlocking *understanding.*

🔋 Energy and Efficiency Link

Accessing large knowledge models requires significant computation power (Watts Family) and optimized chip design (Chip Family).
Modern AIs balance energy efficiency with memory depth — retrieving only the most relevant pieces of knowledge for each prompt.

💬 Quick Takeaway

The Knowledge Family transforms AI from a data processor into a digital thinker.
It's not about memorization — it's about understanding patterns, meaning, and relationships that power intelligent behavior.

⚙️ The Algorithm Family

Definition and Overview

The **Algorithm Family** represents the *thinking engine* of artificial intelligence — the set of mathematical instructions that guide how AI analyzes data, learns patterns, and makes decisions.

An **algorithm** is a sequence of steps designed to solve a problem or complete a task. In AI, algorithms tell the system *how to learn*, *how to predict*, and *how to improve* with every iteration.

In simple terms:

The Algorithm Family is the *logic of intelligence* — the invisible code that transforms data into decisions and predictions into progress.

🧠 How Algorithms Power AI

Every AI system — from simple chatbots to large-scale deep learning models — relies on algorithms as its foundation.
They determine how the model:

- Processes and cleans data,
- Identifies relationships between variables,
- Learns from feedback, and
- Improves over time.

Without algorithms, even the most powerful dataset or neural network would remain static and lifeless.

In essence, **algorithms are the teachers** that train AI how to think.

⚙️ Why the Algorithm Family Matters

Algorithms are what separate automation from intelligence.
They allow machines to **reason**, **adapt**, and **learn** — not just follow commands.
For prompt engineers, understanding algorithmic behavior helps explain *why* AI sometimes misunderstands a question, repeats patterns, or changes tone after feedback.

Every AI response you receive follows an underlying process — a pattern recognition journey from input to output.

🧬 The Algorithm Family Tree

Member	Definition	Purpose	Example Use
Rule-Based Algorithm	Follows predefined logic ("if X, then Y")	Solves predictable problems	Spam filters, decision trees
Search Algorithm	Finds optimal solutions among many options	Guides reasoning and exploration	Pathfinding, optimization
Sorting Algorithm	Organizes data efficiently	Enhances speed and retrieval	Alphabetizing or ranking results
Machine Learning Algorithm	Learns patterns from data without explicit rules	Powers adaptive behavior	Linear regression, decision trees
Deep Learning Algorithm	Learns complex representations from large datasets	Enables vision, speech, and text comprehension	Neural networks, CNNs, RNNs
Reinforcement Learning	Learns by trial and reward feedback	Builds adaptive and goal-oriented systems	Game-playing AI, robotics
Genetic Algorithm	Evolves solutions through mutation and selection	Mimics biological evolution	Design optimization
Clustering Algorithm	Groups similar data points together	Discovers hidden structures	Market segmentation, anomaly detection
Recommendation Algorithm	Predicts user preferences	Personalizes digital experiences	Netflix, YouTube, Amazon suggestions
Optimization Algorithm	Improves efficiency and accuracy of models	Finds best solutions under constraints	Gradient descent, Adam optimizer

🌍 Analogy for Everyday Readers

Imagine AI as a chef in a kitchen:

- The **Dataset Family** provides the ingredients.
- The **Knowledge Family** gives the recipes.
- The **Algorithm Family** is the *cooking process* — mixing, heating, tasting, and adjusting until the dish is perfect.

Just as cooking methods determine the quality of food, algorithms determine the quality of intelligence.

⚡ Algorithm Efficiency and Energy Use

Not all algorithms are equal.
Some are **fast but shallow**, while others are **deep but energy-intensive**.
Training large AI models requires algorithms that can handle billions of calculations per second — powered by the **Watts Family** (energy) and executed through the **Chip Family** (hardware).

The design of efficient algorithms directly affects sustainability in AI — minimizing power consumption while maximizing accuracy and speed.

🧩 Algorithms and Prompt Engineering

For prompt engineers, algorithms explain *how* the AI arrives at its answers.
When a model gives inconsistent or off-topic results, it's often due to:

- Misinterpretation of input signals (input encoding),
- Bias in training algorithms, or
- Overfitting to certain data patterns.

Knowing this helps you craft prompts that guide the AI's decision-making — not just its output.

💬 Quick Takeaway

The Algorithm Family is the reasoning heart of AI.
It transforms information into understanding and enables machines to think, learn, and evolve like digital problem-solvers.

🔢 The Logic Family

Definition and Overview

The **Logic Family** represents the *reasoning framework* of artificial intelligence — the system of rules and operations that helps AI evaluate truth, make deductions, and connect cause and effect.

In AI, logic is not emotion or instinct. It is a formal structure — a system of "if-then" reasoning that allows machines to process information consistently and rationally.

In simple terms:

The Logic Family is the *blueprint of rational thought* — it teaches AI how to reason, compare, infer, and decide.

⚙ Why the Logic Family Matters

Logic gives AI its discipline. It's what makes an AI system trustworthy, explainable, and consistent.
While algorithms help AI *learn patterns*, logic helps it *validate those patterns.*

For prompt engineers, understanding logic is essential because every well-structured prompt contains a logical flow — a beginning, a condition, and an expected outcome.

Without logical structure, even a well-trained AI produces vague or irrelevant results.

How Logic Powers AI

AI applies logic in every decision it makes:

- It checks conditions (if X, then Y).
- It combines facts (A and B are true).
- It eliminates contradictions (A cannot be both true and false).
- It evaluates relationships (if A causes B, what happens next?).

Logic also underpins **machine learning interpretability** — helping explain why AI models make certain predictions and how they reach conclusions.

The Logic Family Tree

Member	Definition	Purpose	Example Use
Boolean Logic	Uses TRUE/FALSE values to represent decisions	Foundational logic system for all computing	if (x > y) return true
Propositional Logic	Analyzes statements that can be true or false	Simplifies reasoning into yes/no forms	"If it rains, then the ground is wet."
Predicate Logic	Works with variables and relationships	Enables AI to reason about objects and their properties	"All cats are mammals. Felix is a cat. Therefore, Felix is a mammal."
Fuzzy Logic	Allows partial truths (degrees of truth)	Models uncertainty and nuance	"The water is somewhat warm."
Modal Logic	Considers possibility and necessity	Used in decision-making under uncertainty	"It is possible that X will happen."
Temporal Logic	Evaluates sequences and timing of events	Useful in automation and robotics	"If button A is pressed, then light B turns on after 3 seconds."
Non-Monotonic Logic	Adapts conclusions as new information appears	Mirrors human-like flexibility	"If birds fly, but penguins don't, update the rule."

Member	Definition	Purpose	Example Use
Deductive Logic	Moves from general principles to specific conclusions	Ensures consistency and truthfulness	Law and policy automation
Inductive Logic	Draws general rules from specific examples	Supports machine learning and prediction	Data-driven trend analysis
Abductive Logic	Infers the most likely explanation	Powers AI reasoning and problem-solving	Diagnosing a likely cause of an event

🌍 Analogy for Everyday Readers

Imagine AI as a detective:

- **Algorithms** are the detective's tools.
- **Logic** is the detective's reasoning process.

Logic helps the AI connect the dots — finding clues, testing hypotheses, and ruling out impossible conclusions until only the most probable truth remains.

That's how AI transforms data into decisions.

⚡ Logic and Prompt Engineering

A powerful prompt always follows a **logical sequence**:

1. Define the role ("You are a data analyst...")
2. State the goal ("Analyze the following numbers...")
3. Provide conditions ("Focus on values above 80...")
4. Request output ("Summarize findings in bullet points.")

This structure mirrors the way logic operates inside AI — **condition, action, result.** When prompts follow logical order, the AI understands and responds with clarity and precision.

🔋 Logic, Energy, and Efficiency

Logical reasoning allows AI to *avoid unnecessary computations.*
By applying logic trees and decision rules, AI reduces energy waste (Watts Family) and computational load (Chip Family).
It's not just smarter — it's greener and faster.

💬 Quick Takeaway

The Logic Family gives AI its reasoning power.
It ensures that intelligence is not only powerful — but also rational, explainable, and trustworthy.

The Language Family

Definition and Overview

The **Language Family** represents the *communication bridge* between humans and artificial intelligence.
It's the system that allows machines to understand, interpret, and generate human language through symbols, syntax, and meaning.

In essence:

The Language Family is the *soul of interaction* — where words become intelligence, and intelligence becomes conversation.

Language is how humans express thought — and now, it's how we teach machines to think, reason, and create.
Through the power of natural language processing (NLP), AI systems can translate, summarize, answer questions, tell stories, and even hold complex dialogues.

Every word you type, every sentence you craft — it all passes through this family before becoming an AI response.

⚙️ Why the Language Family Matters

The Language Family is the foundation of **prompt engineering.**
Without it, communication between humans and machines would be impossible.

AI doesn't "understand" words like we do — it *mathematically interprets them.*
Each word is converted into a **vector**, a numerical representation that captures meaning, tone, and context.
Through this process, the AI learns how words relate to each other — just as humans learn through patterns and experience.

Language is what turns your prompt — a few lines of text — into a full conversation of understanding, logic, and creativity.

🧠 How the Language Family Works

The Language Family operates across multiple layers of comprehension:

1. **Syntax (Structure):** Understanding grammar and sentence order.
2. **Semantics (Meaning):** Understanding what the words mean.
3. **Pragmatics (Context):** Understanding what you *intend* to say.
4. **Emotion and Tone:** Understanding how you want it to *feel.*

Together, these elements allow AI to interpret nuance — the difference between a question, a command, and a creative request.

🧬 The Language Family Tree

Member	Definition	Purpose	Example Use
Natural Language Processing (NLP)	Enables machines to understand human language	Core of all text-based AI	Chatbots, search engines
Natural Language Understanding (NLU)	Helps AI comprehend meaning and intent	Powers reasoning and context	Virtual assistants, summarization
Natural Language Generation (NLG)	Allows AI to produce human-like text	Creates clear, fluent communication	Content writing, storytelling
Speech Recognition	Converts spoken language into text	Bridges voice and text input	Siri, Alexa, Google Assistant
Speech Synthesis (TTS)	Converts text into spoken language	Gives AI a human-like voice	Audio narration, voicebots
Tokenization	Breaks text into smaller units (tokens)	Helps AI process language efficiently	"I love AI" → [I] [love] [AI]
Embedding Models	Represents meaning as numerical patterns	Captures relationships between words	Word2Vec, BERT embeddings
Language Models (LLMs)	Predict and generate coherent text	Powers systems like GPT, Gemini, Claude	Conversational AI and creative writing
Multilingual Models	Understands and translates multiple languages	Expands global communication	AI translators and localization tools
Sentiment Analysis	Detects emotions and tone in language	Measures human response and feeling	Brand monitoring, empathy AI

🌍 Analogy for Everyday Readers

Think of **The Language Family** as *AI's voice and ears.*
It listens through input (reading your words) and speaks through output (writing its responses).
It's the interpreter between human thought and machine intelligence — making it possible for you to say,

"Write me a business plan,"
and receive an answer that sounds natural, thoughtful, and relevant.

Just as humans grow fluent in new languages, AI grows fluent in human communication.

⚡ Language and the Power of Prompts

Prompt engineering exists *because* of the Language Family.
When you learn to speak clearly to AI — through tone, structure, and clarity — you're essentially learning the **grammar of collaboration.**

The more precise and expressive your language, the more intelligent the AI becomes in return.
That's why prompt engineers are, at their core, **linguists of the digital age.**

🔋 Energy and Intelligence Connection

Processing language requires enormous computational power — billions of parameters working together to understand human text.
That's why energy-efficient chips (Chip Family) and optimized algorithms (Algorithm Family) are essential for real-time communication between humans and AI.
Language is not just words — it's *data in motion.*

💬 Quick Takeaway

The Language Family is where humanity meets intelligence.
It's the reason AI doesn't just compute — it converses.
And when humans learn to speak its language fluently, they unlock the full power of artificial intelligence.

🔝 Top 10 Chips / Chip Families (2025 Edition)

Here's a list of widely known, influential chip families (or chip types) that are relevant in AI, computing, and system design. You can use this list as a reference in your book:

#	Chip / Chip Family	Highlights / Relevance
1	**NVIDIA CUDA GPUs (e.g. A100, H100, RTX series)**	Widely used for AI model training and inference; excellent for parallel matrix math and deep learning.
2	**Google TPU (Tensor Processing Units)**	Specialized AI accelerators built for TensorFlow workloads; high performance per watt for neural networks.
3	**Apple M-series (M1, M2, M3 with Neural Engine)**	Integrated SoC combining CPU, GPU, and neural engine; good for on-device AI tasks and low-latency inference.
4	**AMD Instinct / Radeon Accelerators**	Competes in AI compute and HPC (high-performance computing) spaces; open driver ecosystem.
5	**Intel Xeon + Gaudi / Habana chips**	Server-grade CPUs paired with AI accelerators (Habana) for enterprise-scale AI workloads.
6	**Arm Compute / Arm NPUs (Neural Processing Units)**	Low-power accelerators embedded in mobile and IoT devices for edge AI inference.
7	**Tesla FSD / Tesla Dojo Chips**	Custom chips designed specifically for autonomous driving and real-time sensor processing.
8	**Graphcore IPU (Intelligence Processing Unit)**	Designed for graph and neural network workloads; efficient for sparse operations and GNNs.
9	**Xilinx / AMD FPGA (Field-Programmable Gate Arrays)**	Programmable chips that can be customized for AI kernels, inference pipelines, or hardware acceleration.
10	**Cerebras Wafer-Scale Engine (WSE)**	Massive, high-bandwidth AI chip designed for training very large models at scale.

How AI Understands Human Language

Artificial Intelligence doesn't truly *understand* human language the way people do. Instead, it uses advanced mathematics, pattern recognition, and probability to interpret meaning from our words. When we speak or type, AI converts our sentences into a format it can process — a numerical language of its own.

The process begins with **tokenization**, where every word, punctuation mark, or symbol is broken down into smaller pieces called *tokens*. These tokens are then translated into **vectors** — lists of numbers that capture the relationships and meanings between words. Through this transformation, words like *"teacher," "student,"* and *"school"* become mathematically related within the AI's model of language.

Once the words are represented as numbers, the information passes through a **neural network**, an intricate system of layers that identify grammar, meaning, and emotional tone. Modern AI models use what is known as the **Transformer architecture**, which allows them to analyze all words in a sentence simultaneously to determine their context. This means AI can tell whether the word *"bank"* refers to a financial institution or the side of a river based on the other words in the sentence.

After understanding context, the AI begins **predicting** what comes next by calculating probabilities for each possible word or phrase. The result is a response that appears natural and thoughtful — not because the AI feels or reasons like a human, but because it has learned from patterns found in vast amounts of text.

In essence, AI turns human language into numbers, studies patterns within those numbers, and converts the results back into sentences that sound human. It doesn't "think" — it **recognizes**, **predicts**, and **responds** based on everything it has learned.

In Simple Terms

Raw text = **Your words before meaning is attached.**
Tokens = **Broken pieces of those words.**
Embeddings = **Numbers representing those pieces.**
Response = **AI's best prediction of what those words mean in context.**

Front End of AI

The **front end** is the *visible side* — the part you, the user, directly interact with.
It includes things like:

- The chat box where you type your questions
- The "Send" button you click
- Voice or microphone input if you speak
- The AI's written or spoken reply that appears on your screen

All these belong to the *front end*, just like the front of a website or an app.
It's the **human–AI communication layer.**

What Happens in the Front End

When you type something like:

"Explain what raw text means in AI."

1. **Your message** is captured as *raw text* by the front end.
2. That raw text is **sent to the AI model** (the *back end*).
3. The *back end* analyzes the text using algorithms and neural networks.
4. The *front end* then displays the AI's response back to you.

Simple Analogy

Think of it like ordering at a restaurant:

- The **front end** is the waiter who takes your order (your words).
- The **back end** is the kitchen where chefs (AI models) process and prepare the food (the response).
- Then the waiter (front end) brings it back to your table.

So yes — when you talk to AI and it receives your words as **raw text**, that interaction is happening on the **front end**, before the message travels deeper into the **back end**, where real computation and reasoning occur.

🧠 Step 1: Input — Humans Speak or Type

When you type or say something like:

"Write me a poem about love,"
the AI first receives it as **raw text** — just a sequence of words, characters, and symbols.

Example:
`["Write", "me", "a", "poem", "about", "love"]`

🔡 Step 2: Tokenization

AI breaks your sentence into **tokens** (small units of meaning).
Tokens can be whole words, parts of words, or even punctuation marks.

For example:

"Write me a poem about love."
becomes → `[Write] [me] [a] [poem] [about] [love] [.]`

This process lets the AI handle language mathematically — like numbers instead of words.

🔢 Step 3: Numerical Encoding (Vectors)

Each token is converted into a **vector** — a list of numbers representing meaning, context, and relationships between words.

Think of it like this:

- "King" might become `[0.2, 0.8, 0.5, 0.9]`
- "Queen" might become `[0.2, 0.8, 0.6, 0.8]`

These numbers capture **semantic relationships**, so the AI "knows" that *King* and *Queen* are related concepts.

🧩 Step 4: Pattern Recognition via Neural Networks

Now the magic happens.
The AI runs your tokenized, vectorized sentence through layers of a **neural network**, which looks for **patterns** it has seen during training.

Each layer:

- Detects grammar structure ("who did what to whom")
- Recognizes meaning ("poem about love" → it's a creative task)
- Predicts what's likely to come next

This is called **Deep Learning** — thousands of layers transforming patterns of numbers into meaning.

🧭 Step 5: Contextual Understanding

The AI uses a **Transformer architecture** (the "T" in ChatGPT).
It looks at **all words in your sentence at once**, not just one by one, to understand context.

For example:

- "Bank" could mean *riverbank* or *money bank.*
- The AI looks at surrounding words to decide which meaning fits:
    - "I sat by the **bank** of the river." → river
    - "I went to the **bank** to deposit money." → finance

That's called **attention mechanism** — it helps AI focus on the right meaning.

💬 Step 6: Output Generation

After processing, the AI starts to **predict** the most likely next token — word by word, or token by token.

It doesn't "know" the answer; it *calculates probabilities*:

"Write me a poem about love."
Might lead to predictions like:

- "Love" → 0.92 probability
- "is" → 0.85
- "like" → 0.77
- "the sun" → 0.65

So the AI might generate:

"Love is like the sun that warms the soul."

🔄 Step 7: Feedback & Refinement

In interactive systems (like ChatGPT or your AI Agents), the AI adjusts its response based on **your feedback** or **conversation history** — learning the style, tone, or focus you want.

🧩 Summary

Step	What Happens	AI's Role
1. Input	You type or speak words	Receives raw text
2. Tokenization	Splits into parts	Breaks text into units
3. Encoding	Turns tokens into numbers	Represents meaning in math
4. Pattern Recognition	Neural networks process data	Finds grammar and meaning
5. Context Understanding	Transformer model focuses on words	Chooses correct sense or tone
6. Output	AI predicts words	Generates human-like text
7. Feedback	You react, AI refines	Learns your intent better

💡 **In short:**
AI doesn't truly *understand* words like humans do — it *maps patterns between words, meanings, and contexts* it has learned from billions of examples.

🍀 The Ingredients in the Back End of AI

Just like a chef needs ingredients to prepare a meal, AI needs key elements in its back end to process, understand, and respond. These "ingredients" work together to make artificial intelligence function smoothly and intelligently.

1. Data

Data is the **main ingredient** — the foundation of everything AI knows.
AI models are trained on vast amounts of text, images, code, and more.
This includes books, websites, conversations, and open-source materials.
The more diverse and accurate the data, the smarter and more reliable the AI becomes.

📘 *Think of data as the ingredients in a recipe — without them, you can't cook anything.*

2. Algorithms

Algorithms are the **step-by-step instructions** that tell the AI how to learn, analyze, and respond.
They guide how data is processed, how predictions are made, and how the model improves over time.
Examples include **gradient descent**, **backpropagation**, and **transformer architectures**.

📘 *If data is the ingredient, algorithms are the cooking method.*

3. Neural Networks

Neural networks are **the brain of the back end**.
They're layers of interconnected nodes (called neurons) that simulate how human brains process information.
Each layer refines the understanding — from recognizing letters, to words, to entire meanings.

📘 *They are like the chef's brain that decides how to mix the ingredients to make the perfect dish.*

4. Machine Learning Models

These are the **trained systems** that actually perform the tasks — like ChatGPT, Gemini, Claude, or Copilot.
A model is the result of feeding data through algorithms and neural networks until it learns patterns.
Each model has a different purpose: text generation, translation, image recognition, or speech analysis.

📘 *Think of this as the final recipe created after many rounds of tasting and testing.*

5. Training and Optimization

Before an AI model can be used, it goes through **training** — the process of learning from data.
Optimization fine-tunes the model's performance to make it faster, more accurate, and less biased.

📘 *Training is like practice — the chef trying many versions of the same dish until it's perfect.*

6. Infrastructure (Hardware and Software)

Behind every AI system are powerful **computers, GPUs, and servers** that handle all the calculations.
Frameworks like **TensorFlow**, **PyTorch**, and **JAX** act as the tools that hold everything together.

📘 *These are the kitchen appliances and tools — ovens, mixers, and knives — that make cooking possible.*

7. Databases and Storage

All the data and learned information are stored in **databases** or **cloud storage systems**. These allow the AI to retrieve patterns or examples instantly when you ask a question.

📘 *This is the pantry where all the ingredients are kept and organized.*

8. APIs and Middleware

APIs (Application Programming Interfaces) connect the back end to the front end.
They are the **communication pipes** that let your words flow to the AI engine and the answers come back.

📘 *They're like the waiter delivering dishes from the kitchen to your table.*

🧠 In Summary

The back end of AI is made up of these 8 essential ingredients:
1 Data
2 Algorithms
3 Neural Networks
4 Machine Learning Models
5 Training and Optimization
6 Infrastructure
7 Databases and Storage
8 APIs and Middleware

Together, they form the unseen but powerful system that turns **raw text** into **meaningful, intelligent responses.**

Why I Wrote This Book

When I first began talking to AI, I realized something profound — the quality of the answer always depended on the quality of the question.

Every interaction was like holding a mirror to my thoughts. The clearer and more intentional my question became, the more intelligent, creative, and useful the AI's response was. It wasn't about knowing everything — it was about learning how to ask.

That realization changed everything.

From publishing five books to building three eCommerce websites, AI became my silent partner — brainstorming, designing, researching, and simplifying what once felt impossible. But none of it would have worked without understanding one essential skill: **prompting**.

Prompting is more than typing words into a box. It's the **art of communication with intelligence.**
It's how you transform a machine into a creative collaborator, a research assistant, a teacher, or even a visionary partner who helps you build what you once only dreamed of.

This book exists because I've seen the difference that **good prompts** make — not just in business or writing, but in thinking. AI can amplify human creativity, but only when we speak its language. Prompting is that language.

I've experienced incredible results simply by knowing how to ask the right questions. With one prompt, I've built full websites. With another, I've outlined books, created business plans, designed products, and even solved technical problems I didn't know how to begin.

That's the power I want to share with you.

Prompting gives you **clarity**, **confidence**, and **control** — it bridges human creativity and artificial intelligence. Whether you're a teacher, entrepreneur, student, or dreamer, this book will show you how to think differently, ask better questions, and unlock possibilities you never thought possible.

Because when you know what to say when you talk to AI, you're not just giving instructions —
you're **starting a conversation with the future.**

Author's Reflection

When I began my journey into AI, I wasn't trying to become a programmer or a technologist — I was simply curious. I wanted to understand, to create, and to communicate better.

Over time, I realized that AI isn't just a tool — it's a partner that listens, learns, and reflects your thoughts back to you. The moment I learned how to ask better questions, AI began to give me better answers — not just in words, but in ideas, in structure, and in clarity.

This is my sixth book and part of a much larger vision that now includes three growing eCommerce sites. Every one of them began with a single prompt — a conversation with AI that led to creation. Each book, each project, each idea was born from curiosity and refined through communication.

AI helped me dream bigger, think deeper, and work faster. But what truly changed everything was the realization that **the key to unlocking AI's full potential is the human behind the prompt.**

We are living in an extraordinary time — one where words can move systems, design solutions, and even build businesses. But only if we know how to use them.

So this book is not just about prompts.
It's about **human connection**, **clarity of thought**, and **creative leadership** in the age of intelligence.
Because AI will only ever be as powerful as the questions we dare to ask.

What to Say When I Talk to AI: Prompt Engineering Guide

Chapter 1 — Unlocking AI: The Art and Science of Prompt Engineering

From confusion to clarity — learning what to say when you talk to AI

The Conversation That Changed Everything

Three years ago, I sat at my desk staring at an unfamiliar AI chat window.
On the screen glowed a simple prompt box and a blinking cursor promising limitless possibility.
I had built e-commerce sites, written books on AI terminology and no-code design, and trained digital agents for real businesses.
I thought I knew technology.
Then I typed:

Make me a marketing plan.

Seconds later the AI answered politely but mechanically, spitting out a generic outline that could have applied to any company in the world.
It felt like asking a chef to cook dinner and receiving a printout of the food pyramid.

So I tried again:

Create a better marketing plan.

The answer was longer but not wiser.
That was the moment I realized that the problem wasn't the AI's intelligence — it was my **language**.
I was speaking to the machine the way I'd speak to Google, not the way you speak to a collaborator.

That moment became the seed of this book.
It taught me that success with AI depends less on technical power and more on **how you talk to it**.

Why Prompt Engineering Matters

Prompt engineering is the missing literacy of the AI era—the bridge between human intention and machine interpretation.

At its core, a *prompt* is nothing more than an instruction: a request written in natural language that tells an AI model what to do. But the **structure** and **clarity** of that request decide everything about the result.

You can think of it like photography. A world-class camera cannot make you a photographer. It captures whatever you aim at—and if your framing is poor or your focus soft, even the best sensor will produce a bad shot. Likewise, a large-language model like GPT or Gemini captures the "frame" you describe in your prompt. If the picture in your words is fuzzy, your results will be too.

Prompt engineering turns casual users into skilled communicators who know how to aim the lens, adjust the lighting, and compose the scene. It is not about tricking AI—it is about **collaborating intentionally**.

When you master prompting, you stop asking *for* answers and start designing *outcomes.*

The Hidden Cost of Poor Prompting

Every weak prompt carries a hidden cost.

- **Time Drain:** Unclear wording forces you into endless rewrites. Ten minutes of work becomes an hour of repairs.
- **Generic Results:** Without specifics, the model fills gaps with the most common answers it has seen.
- **Quality Risks:** Ambiguous instructions can produce inaccurate or off-brand material that damages credibility.
- **Confidence Loss:** After several disappointing attempts, people conclude that "AI just doesn't work." They stop experimenting—right before the breakthrough would have come.

I have watched organizations spend thousands on AI subscriptions but achieve little because their teams never learned to *talk to the tool.* The problem was never intelligence. The problem was *communication.*

How AI Really Understands You

AI does not "understand" language the way humans do. It doesn't feel, believe, or reason. Instead, it processes words as **tokens**—tiny fragments of meaning like *mar*, *ket*, *ing.* Each token is assigned probabilities based on patterns learned from billions of texts. When you type a sentence, the model predicts the next most likely token, again and again, until it forms a reply.

That means clarity isn't optional; it's everything. A vague request opens an enormous probability cloud. A precise prompt narrows that cloud to a laser beam.

Compare these two:

"Write a marketing plan."
"Write a 30-day marketing plan for a neighborhood bakery specializing in sourdough bread. Focus on weekend promotions and low-budget social media ads."

The first leaves the model guessing; the second gives it a map.
Prompt engineering is the skill of shrinking uncertainty until the machine's probabilities align with your purpose.

The Language Behind the Machine

Beneath every AI conversation lies a vast linguistic engine. Modern models convert words into mathematical *vectors*—rows of numbers representing meaning in many dimensions. Words used in similar contexts occupy similar positions in this invisible space, a process called **embedding.**

When you add context to a prompt—audience, tone, or goal—you shift those vectors closer to the cluster of examples that fit your intent. The model then draws from that region to generate text. In essence, you are not asking the AI to think; you are **steering it through a landscape of language.**

This is why phrasing, order, and even punctuation can influence results. Each variation changes the coordinates of meaning. To the model, "Explain the problem clearly" and "Give a clear explanation of the problem" are not identical—they occupy slightly different spots in semantic space.

Good prompt engineers learn to *feel* these subtle shifts. They know when to add examples, when to use constraints, and when to let the model roam creatively.

The Psychology of a Good Prompt

If mathematics governs the machine, psychology governs the human side of prompting. Three principles connect them:

1. **Framing.** Questions framed positively invite constructive answers. Instead of "Why is this wrong?" try "How can this be improved?"
2. **Role Priming.** Assigning the AI a role—teacher, strategist, analyst—focuses its responses. Roles provide perspective.
3. **Cognitive Load.** Short, focused requests outperform overloaded ones. Divide big tasks into smaller steps; you'll gain clarity and control.

Prompt engineering, at its best, is empathy in technical form. You imagine what the system needs to interpret you correctly, then you meet it halfway.

The 4 C's Framework of Prompt Engineering

Through hundreds of experiments, I distilled effective prompting into four pillars—the **4 C's**:

1. **Clarity** – State precisely what you need.
2. **Context** – Give background, goals, and audience.
3. **Constraints** – Define boundaries such as tone, length, or format.
4. **Creativity** – Invite exploration and variety.

Each one amplifies the others. Together they transform AI from a guessing engine into a thinking partner.

Example:

Weak Prompt: "Write ideas for a children's book."
Strong Prompt: "You are a children's author. Create three story ideas for readers aged 7–9 that teach friendship and resilience. Write in a warm, imaginative tone similar to Roald Dahl."

The difference isn't just wording; it's structure. The second contains all 4 C's—and the AI responds in kind.

Applying the 4 C's

When you learn to combine clarity, context, constraints, and creativity, you move from asking for content to designing collaboration.
A good prompt becomes a **conversation script**, guiding the model through reasoning, tone, and purpose.

Inside later chapters, we'll explore how each C operates in specific fields—from marketing campaigns to technical documentation—but for now, remember this:

Every prompt is a mirror. The AI reflects the precision and intention you bring to it.

What to Say When You Talk to AI: A Prompt AI Engineering Guide

The 4 C's in Action

Each of the 4 C's works like a lens that sharpens communication between you and AI. When combined, they create balance — clarity gives direction, context adds depth, constraints provide focus, and creativity keeps ideas fresh.

1. Clarity — State Precisely What You Need

Definition:
Clarity eliminates confusion. A clear prompt uses direct language, avoids ambiguity, and tells the AI *exactly* what to produce.

Weak Prompt:

"Write something about climate change."

Strong Prompt (with clarity):

"Write a 200-word overview explaining the main causes of climate change, focusing on human activity and its impact on ocean temperatures."

Why it works:
The AI now knows the *topic* (climate change), *scope* (causes and human impact), and *length* (200 words).
Clarity converts uncertainty into precision — it tells the model *where to aim.*

2. Context — Give Background, Goals, and Audience

Definition:
Context teaches the AI *who it's talking to* and *why* the response matters. Without context, the model can't adapt tone or depth.

Weak Prompt:

"Explain machine learning."

Strong Prompt (with context):

"You are a high school computer science teacher. Explain machine learning to 11th-grade students using simple analogies, like teaching a dog new tricks."

Why it works:
Context defines the *role* (teacher), *audience* (students), and *style* (simple, analogy-based). This lets the AI tailor its response to be educational and age-appropriate instead of academic or overly technical.

3. Constraints — Define Boundaries Such as Tone, Length, or Format

Definition:
Constraints guide the shape of the output. They tell AI *how* to respond, not just *what* to say.
Without constraints, AI often gives too much or too little information.

Weak Prompt:

"Write an article about time management."

Strong Prompt (with constraints):

"Write a 500-word blog post about time management for busy entrepreneurs. Use bullet points, short paragraphs, and a motivational tone."

Why it works:
The AI now knows the *length* (500 words), *format* (blog with bullet points), *audience* (entrepreneurs), and *tone* (motivational).
Constraints act like guardrails, keeping the response structured and usable.

4. Creativity — Invite Exploration and Variety

Definition:
Creativity invites the AI to explore possibilities within your guidelines.
It transforms ordinary tasks into opportunities for innovation.

Weak Prompt:

"Write a story about a hero."

Strong Prompt (with creativity):

"Write a short story about a shy librarian who discovers she can time-travel through books. Use humor, emotional depth, and an inspiring ending."

Why it works:
You've given the AI freedom (*humor, emotional depth, imaginative concept*) within gentle boundaries.
This balance produces a unique, engaging response instead of a generic one.

Bringing It All Together

Let's see how all four C's combine in a single, well-engineered prompt.

Weak Prompt:

"Write a social media post for my business."

Strong Prompt (All 4 C's):

"You are a digital marketing expert. Write a 60-word Instagram post for a handmade jewelry business targeting young adults who love eco-friendly products. Use a friendly, conversational tone and include one creative call-to-action."

How it works:

- **Clarity:** Specifies *what* to write (Instagram post).
- **Context:** Defines *who it's for* (eco-conscious young adults).
- **Constraints:** Limits word count, tone, and format.
- **Creativity:** Invites a fun, engaging call-to-action.

Each "C" fine-tunes the output until it feels human, intentional, and useful.

Final Takeaway

Prompting is not about commanding AI — it's about composing a conversation.
When you apply the 4 C's, you become not just a user of AI, but a designer of dialogue.

Mastering the 4 C's is where the journey begins — but to truly understand *why* they work, we need to look deeper. Every prompt you write is part of a long story — the story of how humans have learned to communicate with machines. From the earliest experiments to the breakthroughs of today, prompting has evolved from simple commands into a sophisticated form of collaboration. What you type into an AI system today is built upon decades of progress in language, psychology, and computation.

Understanding this evolution helps you see that prompt engineering is not just a technique — it's the next chapter in how humans teach, guide, and inspire intelligent systems to think with us.

Unlocking AI: The Art and Science of Prompt Engineering

The Evolution of AI Communication

Long before ChatGPT, Bard, and Claude, there was ELIZA—a 1960s computer program created at MIT that simulated a psychotherapist.
ELIZA didn't understand language; it simply mirrored key phrases back at users.
Yet people felt heard. That illusion of understanding revealed something profound: humans naturally fill in the gaps when machines "talk."

Fast-forward to the 1990s and early 2000s.
Voice assistants like Siri, Alexa, and Cortana emerged, blending scripted responses with narrow domain knowledge.
They could answer trivia but stumbled on open-ended reasoning.

Then came the transformer revolution in 2017.
With new architectures and massive datasets, AI began to understand relationships between words instead of treating them as isolated pieces.
For the first time, machines could respond contextually, generating language that felt human.

This shift from rule-based systems to probabilistic reasoning made prompting essential.
The same model could produce brilliant or broken answers—depending entirely on how it was asked.

Communication became the new programming.

Case Studies in Prompt Failure and Fixing

To understand the power of well-crafted prompts, let's look at three quick real-world scenarios.

Case Study 1 — Marketing Makeover
Weak Prompt:
"Write a post to sell my new product."
Result: Generic phrases like "Get yours today!" with no brand voice or emotion.
Fixed Prompt:
"Act as a digital marketing expert. Write a Facebook post for a new eco-friendly water bottle brand called 'OceanSip.'
Target environment-conscious millennials, use a friendly and inspirational tone, and limit to 70 words."
Outcome:
A polished, on-brand post about sustainability and lifestyle.
The difference wasn't the model—it was the clarity of context, role, and constraints.

Case Study 2 — Education in Action
Weak Prompt:
"Explain photosynthesis to a student."
The model returned a dense, textbook paragraph.
Fixed Prompt:
"You are a science teacher for 5th graders. Explain photosynthesis using simple language and a fun example involving a leaf and the sun. Keep it under 150 words."
Now the explanation was clear, playful, and age-appropriate.
Teachers who master prompting like this can personalize lessons instantly.

Case Study 3 — Creative Writing Breakthrough
Weak Prompt:
"Write a story about a robot."
Result: A flat, predictable plot.
Fixed Prompt:
"Write a short story about a robot who teaches children how to dream. Use a warm, emotional tone and end with a lesson about imagination over perfection."
The story transformed from mechanical to magical.
Prompt engineering isn't just for data—it's a bridge between logic and creativity.

Each of these case studies reveals something extraordinary: prompting isn't just about wording — it's about *thinking*. Behind every successful prompt is a human mind organizing ideas, intentions, and empathy into a single clear message.

When you craft a great prompt, you're not programming a machine — you're communicating with a system that reflects your logic, your tone, and even your imagination. AI becomes your mirror, and your words become the lens that shapes its reflection.

This is where the real artistry begins. The science of prompting gives you structure, but the psychology of prompting gives you power. Understanding how language, context, and emotional intent shape AI responses transforms you from a user into a creative director — someone who doesn't just request information but orchestrates intelligence.

Beyond Technique: The Human Mind Behind Every Prompt

Each of these case studies reveals something extraordinary: prompting isn't just about wording — it's about *thinking.* Behind every successful prompt is a human mind organizing ideas, intentions, and empathy into a single clear message.

When you craft a great prompt, you're not programming a machine — you're communicating with a system that reflects your logic, your tone, and even your imagination. AI becomes your mirror, and your words become the lens that shapes its reflection.

This is where the real artistry begins. The science of prompting gives you structure, but the psychology of prompting gives you power. Understanding how language, context, and emotional intent shape AI responses transforms you from a user into a creative director — someone who doesn't just request information but orchestrates intelligence.

In the next chapter, we'll look beyond syntax and strategy. We'll explore the human intuition behind effective prompting — the invisible connection between your thoughts and the AI's understanding — and how mastering that connection can change not just your results, but the way you think and create forever.

Prompting, then, becomes more than a communication skill — it becomes a new literacy of thought. The moment we realize that every prompt carries both logic and emotion, we begin to see AI as an extension of human expression itself. From this understanding grows a larger question: if words can now shape intelligence, how will they reshape creativity, ethics, and the very meaning of being human?

The Future of Human Creativity in the Age of AI

Every technological revolution forces us to ask what it means to be human.
The printing press democratized knowledge; AI democratizes creation.
With it, a teacher can design custom lesson plans in minutes. A designer can generate visual concepts without a studio. An entrepreneur can launch a brand without an agency.
Yet our uniqueness is not diminished—it's amplified.
Prompt engineering does not replace imagination; it extends it. It translates vision into language the machine can understand.
The next era of innovation belongs to those who combine human intuition with AI precision.
It's not about asking the right question once—it's about learning to think in dialogue with intelligence itself.

The Ethics of Communication with AI

As AI becomes a partner in decision-making, ethical prompting matters.
Prompts shape not only answers but values. A biased question yields a biased output.
Learning to write neutral, inclusive prompts is as important as writing accurate ones.

In later chapters, we will explore techniques to audit AI responses and adjust for fairness, but for now, remember:
"The quality of AI ethics begins with the quality of human language."

The New Literacy of the 21st Century

Reading, writing, and arithmetic once defined literacy. Now we add a fourth: reasoning with machines.
Prompt engineering teaches students to express ideas with precision, professionals to delegate intelligently, and creators to expand their imagination through language.
In a world where AI can compose music, analyze contracts, and summarize data, the true competitive advantage is not access—it's articulation.

The Opportunity Ahead

The gap between those who use AI casually and those who use it masterfully will widen dramatically.
Those who learn to "speak AI" will not only work faster—they will think differently.
They will see language as a tool for design, problem-solving, and innovation.
Prompt engineering is the universal translator between human curiosity and machine comprehension.
Master it, and you unlock a new form of power—the power to shape intelligence with your words.

Let's Begin

As you turn the page, we'll move from philosophy to practice—learning how to structure, test, and refine prompts that consistently deliver results.
The future is not about being replaced by AI.
It's about learning what to say when you talk to AI.
Let's begin that conversation—together.

Chapter 2: The Psychology and Design of Prompts — How AI Learns to Think With You

Artificial Intelligence doesn't think like we do — but it learns to **mirror how we think.** Every word you type, every instruction you phrase, becomes a window into your reasoning process. The prompt is not just input; it's a reflection of human cognition — how we process, simplify, and express ideas.

When you talk to AI, you're not giving orders. You're sharing patterns of thought.
The AI responds not to your intention alone, but to the structure and clarity of your expression. The way you organize language tells the machine *how* to think with you — whether to reason, imagine, analyze, or empathize.

In this sense, prompting is more than a tool — it's a **mirror of human consciousness.** It reveals how language carries logic, emotion, and creativity all at once. The better you understand your own thinking, the more clearly AI understands you.

That's why mastering prompts is as much about **self-awareness** as it is about skill. You begin to notice how your tone influences the AI's tone, how your level of detail shapes its focus, and how your curiosity opens new directions in the conversation. Prompting becomes a dialogue between two minds — one human, one synthetic — both learning from the other in real time.

In the pages ahead, we'll explore the **psychological foundations of great prompting:**

- How language framing influences AI reasoning
- How emotion and tone affect creative output
- How human curiosity and clarity drive better results
- And how the art of prompting teaches us more about ourselves than we ever expected

From Understanding to Application

Understanding the psychology of prompting is only the beginning.
Once you know *why* AI reacts the way it does, the next step is learning *how to guide it intentionally.*
Prompt design is where insight turns into action — where self-awareness meets structure.

Think of it as moving from intuition to architecture.
You already know that your words shape the AI's behavior; now you'll learn how to shape them deliberately. Prompt design turns communication into a system — a method you can refine, repeat, and rely on.

Understanding What a Prompt Really Is

Before we dive into techniques and frameworks, we need to establish a clear understanding of what a **prompt** actually is and how AI processes it.

A prompt is **not** a search query. It's **not** a command in the traditional programming sense.
A prompt is a **communication act** — an attempt to convey your intent, requirements, and expectations to a language model in a way that enables it to generate a useful response.

When I first started working with AI, I made the mistake of treating prompts like search engine queries. I would type three or four keywords and expect the AI to read my mind. This approach fails because AI language models do not read minds — they process the specific language you provide and generate responses based on patterns learned from training data.

Think of AI as an **incredibly well-read colleague** who has studied millions of documents but knows nothing about your specific situation unless you explain it. You cannot point at your screen and say *"you know, that thing."* You need to articulate clearly what you want.

The Three Components of Effective Prompts

Through analyzing thousands of successful and failed prompts, I have identified three essential components that effective prompts consistently include:

1. **Intent** – What are you trying to accomplish? What is the end goal?
2. **Specifications** – What specific requirements, constraints, or preferences apply?
3. **Context** – What background information does the AI need to understand your situation?

Let's examine each component in detail.

Intent: The "What" and "Why"

Your intent is the core purpose of your prompt — what you want the AI to produce or help you accomplish.

Weak intent:

"Tell me about marketing."
This is too vague. Marketing is an enormous field. The AI could discuss history, theory, specific tactics, case studies, or hundreds of other aspects. Without clear intent, you'll get a generic response.

Strong intent:

"Explain three digital marketing strategies that work well for B2B software companies with limited budgets."
This intent is specific. It tells the AI exactly what type of information you want, for what context, and with what constraints.

Specifications: The "How"

Specifications define *how* you want the AI to structure, format, or constrain its response.

Weak specifications:

"Make it good."
"Good" is subjective and meaningless to an AI. What qualities define "good" for your purposes?

Strong specifications:

"Present the information as a numbered list with 3–5 bullet points under each strategy explaining implementation steps. Keep the total response under 500 words."

These specifications give the AI clear parameters. It knows the format, structure, level of detail, and length you want.

Context: The "Where" and "Who"

Context provides the background information the AI needs to tailor its response appropriately.

Weak context: None provided.
Without context, AI must make assumptions about your situation, industry, audience, or goals. These assumptions are often wrong.

Strong context:

"I am the marketing director for a 50-person B2B SaaS company selling project management software to construction firms. Our annual marketing budget is limited, and I need strategies I can implement with a small team."

This context transforms the AI's response. Instead of generic advice, you get recommendations tailored to your specific situation.

Putting the Components Together

Let's see how combining these three components transforms a prompt.

Weak prompt:

"Help me with my marketing."
This prompt lacks intent, specifications, and context. The AI must guess at everything. The response will be generic and probably unhelpful.

Strong prompt:

"I am the marketing director for a 50-person B2B SaaS company selling project management software to construction firms. Our annual marketing budget is limited, and I need strategies I can implement with a small team. Explain three digital marketing strategies that work well for companies in my situation, presenting the information as a numbered list with 3–5 bullet points under each strategy explaining implementation steps. Keep the total response under 500 words."

This prompt includes **clear intent** (explain three strategies), **strong specifications** (format, structure, length), and **relevant context** (industry, company size, budget constraints).
The AI can now generate a **useful, targeted response.**

Closing Reflection

By now, you can see that **prompting is both art and architecture**.
It begins with understanding — how AI learns to think with you — and matures through design — how you learn to think deliberately with it.
When psychology and structure work together, your prompts stop being random experiments and become repeatable frameworks for success.

The rest of this book will continue building on that foundation — teaching you how to refine, extend, and personalize your prompts until they reflect not just information, but *intelligence shaped by intention.*

The Three Components of Effective Prompts

Through analyzing thousands of successful and failed prompts, I have identified three essential components that effective prompts consistently include:

Intent. What are you trying to accomplish? What is the end goal?

Specifications. What specific requirements, constraints, or preferences apply?

Context. What background information does the AI need to understand your situation?

Let's examine each component in detail.

Intent: The "What" and "Why"

Your intent is the core purpose of your prompt. What do you want the AI to produce or help you accomplish?

Weak intent: "Tell me about marketing."

This is too vague. Marketing is an enormous field. The AI could discuss history, theory, specific tactics, case studies, or hundreds of other aspects. Without clear intent, you will get a generic response.

Strong intent: "Explain three digital marketing strategies that work well for B2B software companies with limited budgets."

This intent is specific. It tells the AI exactly what type of information you want, for what context, and with what constraints.

Specifications: The "How"

Specifications define how you want the AI to structure, format, or constrain its response.

Weak specifications: "Make it good."

"Good" is subjective and meaningless to an AI. What qualities define "good" for your purposes?

Strong specifications: "Present the information as a numbered list with 3-5 bullet points under each strategy explaining implementation steps. Keep the total response under 500 words."

These specifications give the AI clear parameters. It knows the format, structure, level of detail, and length you want.

Context: The "Where" and "Who"

Context provides the background information the AI needs to tailor its response appropriately.

Weak context: None provided.

Without context, AI must make assumptions about your situation, industry, audience, or goals. These assumptions are often wrong.

Strong context: "I am the marketing director for a 50-person B2B SaaS company selling project management software to construction firms. Our annual marketing budget is limited, and I need strategies I can implement with a small team."

This context transforms the AI's response. Instead of generic advice, you get recommendations tailored to your specific situation.

Putting the Components Together

Let's see how combining these three components transforms a prompt:

Weak prompt: "Help me with my marketing."

This prompt lacks intent, specifications, and context. The AI must guess at everything. The response will be generic and probably unhelpful.

Strong prompt: "I am the marketing director for a 50-person B2B SaaS company selling project management software to construction firms. Our annual marketing budget is limited, and I need strategies I can implement with a small team. Explain three digital marketing strategies that work well for companies in my situation, presenting the information as a numbered list with 3-5 bullet points under each strategy explaining implementation steps. Keep the total response under 500 words."

This prompt includes clear intent (explain three strategies), strong specifications (format, structure, length), and relevant context (industry, company size, budget constraints). The AI can now generate a useful, targeted response.

The Principle of Specificity

One of the most important principles in prompt design is specificity. The more specific your prompt, the more useful the response.

I learned this lesson the hard way while working on "AI Agent Builders." Early in the project, I would ask AI to "describe how an agent works." The responses were technically accurate but uselessly abstract. When I started asking "describe how a customer service AI agent processes an incoming support ticket, including the specific decision points and handoff criteria," the responses became immediately actionable.

Specificity does not mean length. A prompt can be concise and specific. It means being precise about what you want.

Compare these two prompts:

Vague: "Write about employee engagement."

Specific: "Write a 300-word memo to department heads explaining why quarterly employee engagement surveys improve retention, including two specific metrics that demonstrate ROI."

The specific version is only slightly longer but dramatically more precise. It tells the AI the format (memo), audience (department heads), key message (why surveys improve retention), supporting evidence needed (two metrics with ROI), and length (300 words).

Common Prompt Structure Patterns

While prompts can take many forms, certain structures consistently work well. Here are the patterns I use most frequently:

The Direct Instruction Pattern

Structure: [Action verb] + [what] + [specifications]

Example: "Summarize this article in three bullet points, focusing on practical applications for small businesses."

This pattern works well for straightforward tasks where context is either obvious or unnecessary.

The Context-First Pattern

Structure: [Context] + [Intent] + [Specifications]

Example: "I am preparing for a board presentation on Q3 performance. Generate five key talking points highlighting revenue growth and customer acquisition, formatted as slides with a headline and three supporting bullets each."

This pattern works well when your specific situation significantly impacts what good output looks like.

The Example-Enhanced Pattern

Structure: [Intent] + [Example] + [Specifications]

Example: "Write three subject lines for our product launch email. Here is an example of our typical style: 'Your productivity just got smarter—meet the new TaskFlow.' Keep them under 50 characters and maintain a professional but enthusiastic tone."

This pattern works well when you want to match an existing style or format.

The Constrained Pattern

Structure: [Intent] + [What to include] + [What to avoid]

Example: "Explain cloud computing to a non-technical executive. Include concrete business benefits and avoid technical jargon, acronyms, or implementation details."

This pattern works well when you need to navigate specific limitations or requirements.

The Role of Clarity

Clarity is perhaps the most undervalued aspect of prompt design. In my consulting work, I have reviewed hundreds of prompts that failed simply because they were unclear, even when the user knew exactly what they wanted.

Unclear prompts often result from:

Assumed knowledge. You assume the AI knows things it does not—your industry terminology, your company's internal processes, your audience's characteristics.

Ambiguous pronouns. Using "it," "this," "that," "they" without clear antecedents.

Multiple requests in one prompt. Asking for several different things without clearly separating them.

Implied requirements. Expecting the AI to infer unstated constraints or preferences.

Let's examine an unclear prompt and improve it:

Unclear prompt: "Write about it and make it good, with the usual stuff but focus on that thing we discussed."

This prompt might make perfect sense to the human writing it, but the AI has no idea what "it" refers to, what "good" means, what "the usual stuff" includes, or what "that thing" is.

Clear prompt: "Write a 500-word blog post about the benefits of remote work for software developers. Include statistics on productivity and work-life balance, maintain an optimistic but realistic tone, and structure it with an introduction, three main points with supporting evidence, and a conclusion."

This prompt removes all ambiguity. Every requirement is explicit.

Avoiding Common Beginner Mistakes

After teaching prompt engineering to dozens of business professionals, I have noticed that beginners consistently make certain mistakes. Let's address the most common ones:

Mistake 1: The Single-Word Prompt

Example: "Marketing."

What about marketing? This is not a prompt; it is a topic. The AI cannot take action without more information.

Fix: Always include an action verb and specify what you want. "Explain three current trends in digital marketing that apply to B2B companies."

Mistake 2: The Apologetic Prompt

Example: "I'm sorry to bother you, but could you maybe help me with something if you have time? I was wondering if you might be able to possibly..."

AI does not need apologies or softening language. This padding wastes tokens (the units AI uses to process text) and can actually reduce response quality by burying your real request.

Fix: Be direct and confident. "Analyze this data and identify the top three trends."

Mistake 3: The Mind-Reading Prompt

Example: "You know what I mean—do that thing we did last time."

AI has no memory of "last time" unless you are in an ongoing conversation, and even then, it needs explicit references.

Fix: Always provide complete information in each prompt. "Generate a sales email using the format we established: friendly opening, one main value proposition, two supporting benefits, and a clear call to action."

Mistake 4: The Everything Prompt

Example: "Tell me everything about AI, machine learning, neural networks, deep learning, and how to implement them in business, plus give me examples and case studies and also explain the future and ethical considerations."

This prompt asks for a book, not a response. AI responses have practical limits, and trying to cover everything means covering nothing well.

Fix: Break complex requests into focused prompts. Start with "Explain the difference between AI and machine learning in business context, using two examples from different industries."

Mistake 5: The Assumption Prompt

Example: "Improve this" [attaches document without explanation]

Improve how? For what purpose? According to what standards?

Fix: Specify your improvement criteria. "Review this executive summary for clarity and conciseness. Flag any jargon that non-technical readers would not understand and suggest simpler alternatives."

The Iteration Mindset

One of the most important mindset shifts in prompt engineering is accepting that your first prompt will rarely be perfect. Even experts iterate.

When I work with AI tools, my typical process involves:

Initial prompt: My best first attempt based on the frameworks in this chapter.

Response evaluation: Does this meet my needs? If not, what is missing or wrong?

Refined prompt: A more specific version that addresses gaps in the first response.

Response evaluation: Better? If not, what else needs adjustment?

Final prompt: Often my third or fourth attempt, incorporating everything I learned from previous responses.

This iteration is not failure. It is the natural process of refining communication. Think of it like editing a document—your first draft is rarely your final version.

The key is making each iteration strategic, not random. If your first prompt was too vague, add specificity. If it produced content in the wrong format, specify format explicitly. If it missed your intended audience, add context about that audience.

Building Your Prompt Design Intuition

As you practice prompt design, you will develop intuition about what works. Certain patterns will become automatic. You will start anticipating what information AI needs before it fails to deliver what you want.

This intuition comes from two sources:

Volume: Writing many prompts across different use cases.

Analysis: Examining why prompts succeeded or failed.

I recommend keeping a log of your prompts, especially in your early practice. When a prompt works well, note what made it effective. When a prompt fails, note what was missing or unclear.

Over time, patterns will emerge. You will notice that certain types of tasks require certain types of framing. You will develop templates for your common use cases. You will build a personal library of prompt structures that work reliably for your specific needs.

The Foundation Is Set

This chapter established the fundamentals of prompt design: the three components of effective prompts (intent, specifications, context), the principle of specificity, common structure patterns, the importance of clarity, common mistakes to avoid, and the iteration mindset.

These basics form the foundation for everything that follows. The advanced techniques in later chapters all build on these core principles.

In Chapter 3, we will focus specifically on instructional prompts—how to give AI clear, actionable commands that produce the precise results you need.

Chapter 3: Instructional Prompts: Giving Clear Commands

The Nature of Instructions

An instructional prompt is the simplest and most direct form of communication with AI. You tell it what to do, and it does it. Or at least, that is the theory.

In practice, giving effective instructions to AI requires more nuance than many people expect. The challenge is not that AI misunderstands complex instructions—it is that AI interprets vague instructions literally, often in ways that surprise us.

I learned this while developing agent systems. An agent might receive the instruction "handle customer complaints," which sounds clear enough to a human manager. But an AI needs to know: What constitutes a complaint versus a question? What actions count as "handling"? What tone should responses take? When should it escalate to a human?

Without explicit instructions on these points, the AI will make assumptions based on patterns in its training data. Sometimes those assumptions align with your intentions. Often they do not.

The Anatomy of a Clear Instruction

A clear instruction contains four elements:

Action: What specific task should the AI perform?

Subject: What should it perform the task on?

Manner: How should it perform the task?

Outcome: What should the result look like?

Let's see this in practice:

Weak instruction: "Fix this email."

This instruction has only an action (fix) and an implied subject (this email). It lacks manner (how should it be fixed?) and outcome (what should the result look like?).

Strong instruction: "Revise this email to make it more concise and professional. Remove casual language, eliminate redundant phrases, and ensure the main request is clear in the first paragraph. The final version should be 150 words or less."

This instruction specifies:

- Action: Revise
- Subject: This email
- Manner: More concise and professional, remove casual language, eliminate redundancy, make request clear in first paragraph
- Outcome: 150 words or less

The AI now has clear direction on what to do and what success looks like.

Action Verbs Matter

The verb you choose as your action word significantly impacts the response you receive. AI models are trained to recognize that different verbs imply different types of tasks and outputs.

Consider how these different verbs would generate different responses to the same subject:

"Summarize this report" produces a shorter version hitting main points.

"Analyze this report" identifies patterns, trends, and insights.

"Critique this report" points out strengths and weaknesses.

"Explain this report" clarifies complex points for understanding.

"Expand this report" adds more detail and supporting information.

Each verb signals a fundamentally different intent.

In my work building ecommerce sites, I once asked an AI to "improve product descriptions." Half the descriptions came back longer, half came back shorter. The AI interpreted "improve" inconsistently because I had not specified whether improvement meant more compelling, more detailed, more concise, or more SEO-friendly.

When I changed the instruction to "rewrite product descriptions to be more compelling to busy professionals, focusing on time-saving benefits and keeping each description between 50-75 words," the results were consistently strong because the action verb (rewrite) was paired with specific manner and outcome criteria.

Here are action verbs that work well for different types of tasks:

For content creation: Write, draft, compose, generate, create, produce

For modification: Revise, edit, refine, improve, enhance, polish, rewrite

For reduction: Summarize, condense, shorten, simplify, distill

For expansion: Elaborate, expand, detail, develop, extend

For analysis: Analyze, evaluate, assess, examine, investigate, review

For explanation: Explain, clarify, describe, illustrate, demonstrate

For transformation: Convert, transform, translate, adapt, reformulate

Choose your action verb carefully based on what type of output you actually want.

Specifying Manner: The "How"

The manner component of your instruction tells AI how to approach the task. This is where you specify tone, style, perspective, level of detail, and constraints.

Let's examine a basic instruction and see how adding manner specifications transforms it:

Basic instruction: "Write a memo about the new remote work policy."

This will produce a memo, but it might be too formal, too casual, too detailed, or too vague for your needs.

With manner specifications: "Write a memo about the new remote work policy in a professional but approachable tone. Address common employee questions proactively, keep sentences short and scannable, and emphasize the benefits alongside the requirements."

Now the AI has clear guidance on tone (professional but approachable), approach (address questions proactively), style (short, scannable sentences), and balance (benefits and requirements).

Manner specifications I use frequently include:

Tone specifications:

- Professional and formal
- Conversational and approachable
- Enthusiastic and energetic
- Calm and reassuring
- Direct and no-nonsense
- Empathetic and understanding

Style specifications:

- Concise and punchy
- Detailed and thorough
- Academic and cited
- Practical and action-oriented
- Creative and engaging
- Technical and precise

Perspective specifications:

- From the company's viewpoint
- From the customer's viewpoint
- From an objective third party
- From a specific role or position

Detail specifications:

- High-level overview
- Moderate detail with examples
- Comprehensive and exhaustive

- Focused only on X aspects

The more specific your manner requirements, the more aligned the output will be with your needs.

Defining Outcomes: What Success Looks Like

The outcome component specifies what the finished product should look like. This includes length, format, structure, and any specific elements that must be included or excluded.

Weak outcome specification: "Make it good."

"Good" is subjective and unmeasurable. The AI cannot optimize for "good."

Strong outcome specifications:

- "Keep it under 200 words"
- "Structure it with five main sections, each with a clear heading"
- "Include at least two specific examples in each section"
- "End with three actionable next steps"
- "Format it as bullet points, not paragraphs"

These specifications are concrete and measurable. The AI knows exactly what the finished product should include.

When working on "No Code, No Problem," I had to generate numerous examples of technical explanations for non-technical readers. My early attempts produced inconsistent results because I was not specifying outcomes clearly.

Once I started including specifications like "Explain in exactly three paragraphs: 1) what it is in plain language, 2) why it matters for business users, 3) one concrete example of using it," the quality and consistency improved dramatically.

The Power of Constraints

Paradoxically, adding constraints often improves AI outputs. Constraints force the AI to prioritize and focus, rather than generating broad, generic responses.

Effective constraints include:

Length constraints: "In exactly 100 words," "Between 500-750 words," "In no more than three sentences"

Scope constraints: "Focus only on financial impacts," "Discuss only the implementation phase," "Address only the top three issues"

Exclusion constraints: "Without using technical jargon," "Without discussing competitors," "Without mentioning price"

Inclusion constraints: "Must include data from the report," "Must reference all three stakeholder groups," "Must address the concerns raised in the meeting"

Format constraints: "As a numbered list," "As a narrative with no bullet points," "As a decision matrix"

Let's see constraints in action:

Without constraints: "Explain the benefits of our new CRM system."

This prompt could generate a response that is too long, too technical, too generic, or too focused on features rather than benefits.

With constraints: "Explain the benefits of our new CRM system in exactly five bullet points, each 20-30 words. Focus only on time-saving benefits for sales representatives. Avoid technical terminology. Each point must include a concrete example."

These constraints shape the response precisely. The AI knows the exact format (five bullets), length (20-30 words each), focus (time-saving for sales reps), style (non-technical), and content requirements (concrete examples).

Sequencing Instructions for Complex Tasks

When a task involves multiple steps or components, the sequence in which you present instructions matters.

For complex instructions, I follow this sequence:

1. **Context** (if needed): Background information
2. **Primary action**: The main task
3. **Manner specifications**: How to approach it
4. **Outcome specifications**: What the result should look like
5. **Constraints**: Limitations or requirements

Here is an example of well-sequenced instructions:

"Our company is launching a new project management tool for remote teams [context]. Write an announcement email to our current customers [primary action] using an excited but professional tone, emphasizing how this solves their specific pain points around team coordination [manner]. The email should follow our standard format: attention-grabbing subject line, brief problem statement, solution presentation, two key features with benefits, and a clear call to action [outcome]. Keep the total email under 250 words and avoid technical specifications [constraints]."

This sequence gives AI all the information it needs in a logical order that builds from context to specific requirements.

The Precision Principle

One of the most important lessons I learned from working with AI agents is what I call the Precision Principle: AI interprets your instructions literally, not generously.

Humans fill in gaps. If you tell a human colleague to "write it like we usually do," they draw on shared context and past examples to understand what you mean.

AI cannot do this. It has no shared context beyond what you provide in the conversation. If you say "write it like we usually do," the AI will either make its best guess based on patterns in its training data or ask for clarification.

The Precision Principle means:

Say exactly what you mean. Do not rely on implications or assumptions.

Define ambiguous terms. What does "professional" mean in your context? What does "concise" mean?

Specify measurements. Not "short" but "under 200 words." Not "a few examples" but "three examples."

Make exclusions explicit. If you do not want something included, say so directly.

Clarify priorities. If multiple requirements conflict, which takes precedence?

Handling Multiple Instructions

Sometimes you need AI to perform several related tasks. How you structure multiple instructions affects whether AI treats them as connected or separate.

Weak approach: "Write a blog post. Make it SEO-friendly. Include statistics. Add a call to action. Keep it under 800 words. Make it engaging."

This is a string of disconnected commands. It is unclear how they relate or which take priority.

Strong approach: "Write an 800-word SEO-friendly blog post about productivity tools for remote workers. Make it engaging by including two relevant statistics and one brief case study. Structure it with an intro, three main sections with clear headers, and a conclusion with a call to action to try our free trial."

This integrates multiple requirements into a coherent instruction. The AI understands how all the pieces fit together.

When you have truly separate tasks, explicitly number or separate them:

"Please complete three tasks:

1. Summarize this report in five bullet points, focusing on financial impacts.
2. Identify the three main risks discussed in the report.
3. Draft one paragraph recommending whether we should proceed, based only on the information in the report."

This structure makes it clear that these are distinct tasks, each with its own requirements.

Testing Your Instructions

Before using an important instruction in a high-stakes situation, test it. Send the prompt, evaluate the response, and refine.

I test instructions by asking:

Did the AI understand the task? Does the response address what I actually asked for?

Did it follow the manner specifications? Is the tone, style, and approach what I specified?

Did it meet the outcome requirements? Is it the right length, format, and structure?

Did it respect the constraints? Did it avoid what I told it to avoid and include what I required?

Is it useful? Even if technically correct, does it actually solve my problem?

If the answer to any of these questions is no, I refine the instruction and test again. Usually, the problem is that I was not specific enough about one of the four elements: action, subject, manner, or outcome.

Common Instructional Failures and Fixes

Let me share the most common ways instructional prompts fail and how to fix them:

Failure: AI produces content that is too generic

Cause: Insufficient context or constraints

Fix: Add specific details about your situation, audience, or requirements. Replace "Write about leadership" with "Write about leadership challenges specific to first-time managers in fast-growing tech startups."

Failure: AI misses the point of your request

Cause: Unclear primary action or buried intent

Fix: Lead with your main request. Instead of "I need help with something. We have this project. Can you maybe write something?" use "Write a project summary for executive stakeholders."

Failure: AI produces the wrong format

Cause: Unspecified or ambiguous outcome requirements

Fix: Explicitly state format. Instead of "Organize this information" use "Organize this information as a three-column comparison table with headers for Features, Benefits, and Costs."

Failure: AI uses the wrong tone

Cause: Unspecified manner requirements

Fix: Define tone explicitly. Instead of "Write a message to the team" use "Write a message to the team in an upbeat, appreciative tone that acknowledges their hard work."

Failure: AI includes unwanted content

Cause: Failing to specify exclusions

Fix: State what to avoid. Instead of "Explain our pricing" use "Explain our pricing focusing on value, without mentioning competitor prices or discounts."

Instructional Prompt Templates

Based on my work across multiple projects, I have developed templates for common instructional tasks. Here are the most useful:

Content Creation Template: "Write a [type] about [topic] for [audience]. Use a [tone] tone. Include [required elements]. Keep it [length]. Structure it as [format]."

Example: "Write a blog post about time management for busy executives. Use a practical, no-nonsense tone. Include three actionable strategies with examples. Keep it 600-800 words. Structure it with an intro, three main sections with clear headers, and a brief conclusion."

Content Revision Template: "Revise this [content type] to [improvement goal]. Specifically [actions to take]. The result should be [outcome specifications]."

Example: "Revise this product description to be more compelling for enterprise buyers. Specifically emphasize security features, add quantified benefits, and remove casual language. The result should be 100-150 words in a professional but accessible tone."

Analysis Template: "Analyze [subject] for [purpose]. Focus on [specific aspects]. Present your findings as [format]. Include [required elements]."

Example: "Analyze this customer feedback data for patterns in complaints. Focus on product features and service issues. Present your findings as a ranked list of top five issues with frequency counts and representative quotes."

Explanation Template: "Explain [concept] to [audience] in [style]. Cover [scope]. Use [analogies/examples]. Avoid [exclusions]."

Example: "Explain blockchain technology to non-technical business executives in plain language. Cover only the business applications and benefits. Use analogies to familiar business systems. Avoid technical implementation details or cryptography."

These templates provide starting points. Adapt them to your specific needs by filling in the brackets with your requirements.

The Art of Directive Language

Effective instructional prompts use directive language—clear commands that leave no ambiguity about what action to take.

Weak directive language:

- "Maybe you could..."
- "I was thinking perhaps..."
- "If possible..."
- "Try to..."

Strong directive language:

- "Write..."
- "Analyze..."
- "Create..."
- "Revise..."

Directive language is not rude. It is clear. AI does not have feelings that can be hurt by direct instructions. In fact, hedging and softening your language often reduces response quality by introducing ambiguity.

Compare these two instructions:

Hedged: "I was wondering if you might be able to possibly help me write something like a summary, if that makes sense, of this report. Maybe keep it kind of short?"

Direct: "Summarize this report in 200 words."

The direct version is clearer, shorter, and will produce better results.

Building Your Instruction Library

As you develop proficiency with instructional prompts, start building a personal library of instructions that work well for your common tasks.

I maintain a document of my most effective prompts, organized by category:

- Email instructions (announcements, responses, follow-ups)
- Content instructions (blog posts, social media, reports)
- Analysis instructions (data review, feedback analysis, document review)
- Planning instructions (meeting agendas, project outlines, strategy documents)

When I encounter a new task similar to something I have done before, I start with a proven instruction and adapt it. This is far more efficient than crafting each prompt from scratch.

Your instruction library becomes a force multiplier. Instead of spending five minutes figuring out how to phrase a request, you can adapt a tested instruction in thirty seconds.

The Feedback Loop

One final principle for instructional prompts: use AI's responses to improve your instructions.

When an AI response misses the mark, examine what your instruction was missing:

If the content is too vague, you need more specific outcome requirements.

If the tone is wrong, you need clearer manner specifications.

If it includes unwanted elements, you need explicit exclusions.

If it misses key points, you need better context or scope definition.

Each failed prompt teaches you something about how to write better instructions. Pay attention to these lessons. Over time, your first-attempt success rate will increase dramatically.

Moving Forward with Instructions

This chapter focused on the foundation of AI communication: clear, effective instructions. We covered the anatomy of instructions (action, subject, manner, outcome), the importance of action verbs, the power of constraints, how to sequence complex instructions, and common failures with their fixes.

Mastering instructional prompts is essential because they form the basis for all other prompting techniques. The context, examples, and complex structures we will explore in coming chapters all build on the instruction fundamentals covered here.

In Chapter 4, we will explore how adding context transforms your prompts, enabling AI to generate responses tailored to your specific situation rather than generic advice.

Chapter 4: Adding Context to Prompts: Setting the Scene

Why Context Changes Everything

Context is the difference between generic advice and actionable solutions. It is the difference between a response that sounds plausible and one that actually works for your specific situation.

I learned this lesson dramatically while consulting with a mid-size manufacturing company. Their marketing director asked an AI tool to "create a social media strategy." The AI generated a perfectly good generic social media strategy—complete with recommendations for TikTok videos, influencer partnerships, and viral content campaigns.

There was just one problem: this company manufactured industrial valve components for oil refineries. Their buying cycle was eighteen months, their customer base was fifty procurement managers at major energy companies, and their average deal size was two million dollars. TikTok videos were not going to help.

The AI was not wrong. It simply lacked context. When we added context about the industry, customer base, buying cycle, and business model, the AI generated a completely different strategy focused on LinkedIn thought leadership, industry publication partnerships, and account-based marketing. This strategy was actually implementable.

Context is information about your specific situation that shapes how AI should approach your request. Without context, AI defaults to the most common patterns in its training data, which may not apply to your circumstances.

Types of Context That Matter

Not all context is equally useful. Through extensive testing across different business scenarios, I have identified six types of context that most significantly improve AI outputs:

Situational context: What is happening in your specific circumstances?

Audience context: Who will consume or be affected by this output?

Purpose context: Why does this matter? What is the broader goal?

Constraint context: What limitations or requirements apply?

Historical context: What has happened before that informs this situation?

Industry context: What industry-specific factors apply?

Let's examine each type in detail.

Situational Context: Your Specific Circumstances

Situational context describes the particular circumstances you are operating within. This includes your role, your organization, your current challenge, and relevant environmental factors.

Without situational context: "Write a proposal for implementing AI tools in our company."

AI must assume a generic company, generic role, generic use case. The result will be broad and possibly irrelevant.

With situational context: "I am the operations director at a 200-person medical device distributor. We currently handle order processing, inventory tracking, and customer service manually through spreadsheets and email. I need to write a proposal for implementing AI tools that will be reviewed by our cost-conscious CEO who is skeptical of technology investments."

Now AI understands:

- Your role and authority level
- Company size and industry
- Current state of operations
- Specific pain points (manual processes)
- Key stakeholder (cost-conscious, tech-skeptical CEO)

The resulting proposal will address cost concerns, focus on practical efficiency gains, and use language appropriate for a skeptical executive rather than an enthusiastic tech adopter.

Audience Context: Who This Is For

Audience context is perhaps the most transformative type of context you can provide. The same information presented to different audiences requires different language, emphasis, and structure.

I learned this while writing "The Intelligloss." The same AI term might need to be explained completely differently for a technical developer, a business executive, or a general reader. Without audience context, AI defaults to a middle ground that satisfies no one fully.

Without audience context: "Explain machine learning."

This will produce a generic explanation that might be too technical for some readers and too simplistic for others.

With audience context: "Explain machine learning to the board of directors at a traditional manufacturing company. They have no technical background but need to understand whether we should invest in ML capabilities. They care primarily about ROI and competitive advantage."

Now the explanation will:

- Avoid technical terminology
- Focus on business value
- Address investment concerns
- Relate to manufacturing contexts
- Emphasize competitive implications

The same topic, completely different approach, all because of audience context.

Purpose Context: The "Why" Behind Your Request

Purpose context explains why you need this output and what you plan to do with it. This helps AI prioritize the right information and structure content appropriately.

Without purpose context: "Summarize this market research report."

AI will create a generic summary hitting the main points. But what matters most depends on why you need the summary.

With purpose context: "Summarize this market research report for a budget allocation meeting where I need to justify increasing our marketing spend in the Southeast region. Focus on data that supports regional expansion opportunities."

Now AI knows to:

- Emphasize Southeast-specific findings
- Highlight expansion opportunities
- Include data that supports budget justification
- Structure information persuasively

The summary serves your specific purpose rather than just condensing content.

Constraint Context: Your Limitations and Requirements

Constraint context describes the boundaries within which you must operate. These might be budget constraints, time constraints, resource limitations, policy requirements, or technical limitations.

I encountered this while working with a startup that wanted to "improve customer onboarding." Without constraint context, I helped them design an elaborate multi-week onboarding program with personal consultations and custom training materials.

Then they mentioned they had no customer success team, a product that cost $49/month, and customers who expected to be up and running in minutes. The elaborate program was completely unworkable.

With proper constraint context, we designed a completely different solution: an automated email sequence, in-app tooltips, and short video tutorials—all implementable with their existing resources and appropriate for their product price point.

Without constraint context: "Create a training program for our new software."

With constraint context: "Create a training program for our new software that can be delivered entirely online, requires no live instructors, takes new users less than one hour to complete, and costs less than $500 to produce."

These constraints completely reshape what "training program" means. AI will focus on scalable, asynchronous, cost-effective solutions rather than suggesting instructor-led workshops or elaborate video productions.

Historical Context: What Has Happened Before

Historical context provides background about previous attempts, existing practices, or past results that inform current decisions.

Without historical context: "Write a proposal to change our sales commission structure."

With historical context: "Write a proposal to change our sales commission structure. Our previous attempt three years ago created a revolt among the sales team because it reduced their potential earnings. The CEO is open to changes but extremely cautious about team morale impacts. We need a structure that incentivizes new business development while maintaining team satisfaction."

This historical context tells AI:

- There is relevant history to consider
- Previous approaches failed for specific reasons
- Stakeholder concerns are elevated
- The proposal must balance competing priorities

The resulting proposal will address historical concerns proactively rather than repeating past mistakes.

Industry Context: Domain-Specific Factors

Industry context accounts for factors unique to your industry: regulations, norms, buying behaviors, competitive dynamics, or specialized terminology.

Different industries operate by different rules. A customer retention strategy for a B2B software company looks completely different from one for a consumer retail brand, which looks different from one for a healthcare provider. Without industry context, AI cannot account for these differences.

Without industry context: "Develop a customer retention strategy."

With industry context: "Develop a customer retention strategy for a B2B SaaS company in the legal tech space. Our customers are law firms with 10-50 attorneys. Switching costs are high due to workflow integration, but our competitors are aggressive on pricing. The legal industry is relationship-driven and risk-averse, so trust and reliability matter more than innovation."

This industry context tells AI:

- B2B relationships and sales cycles apply
- Customer size and characteristics
- Competitive dynamics (pricing pressure)
- Industry culture (relationship-driven, risk-averse)
- What customers value (trust and reliability over innovation)

The retention strategy will focus on relationship building, demonstrating reliability, and emphasizing switching costs rather than suggesting tactics that work for consumer brands but would fail in this B2B legal context.

How Much Context Is Enough?

A common question I hear is: "How much context should I provide? When is it too much?"

The answer depends on how much the AI needs to understand your situation to generate useful output. Here is my rule of thumb:

Minimal context needed:

- Tasks where your situation is similar to common scenarios
- Requests for general information or standard formats
- Cases where industry or audience context is obvious

Moderate context needed:

- Tasks requiring adaptation to your specific situation
- Requests that could go multiple directions without guidance
- Cases where wrong assumptions would produce unusable output

Extensive context needed:

- Complex strategic questions
- Situations with important constraints or requirements
- Cases where past attempts failed
- Requests involving multiple stakeholders with different priorities

You know you have provided enough context when you could hand your prompt to a knowledgeable colleague and they would understand exactly what you need and why.

You know you have provided too much context when you include information that does not affect how the AI should approach the task.

Structuring Context Effectively

How you present context matters almost as much as what context you provide. Context that is buried in rambling background tends to be ignored or misweighted.

I structure context using one of two approaches:

The Context-First Structure: Present all context upfront, then make your request.

"[Context paragraph establishing situation, audience, constraints, and purpose]. Based on this context, [specific request]."

This works well when context is substantial and you want AI to keep it all in mind while generating the response.

The Integrated Structure: Weave context throughout your request as relevant.

"Write a proposal for [audience context] about [situational context]. The proposal should [outcome specifications considering constraint context] because [purpose context]."

This works well when context naturally aligns with different parts of your instruction.

Choose whichever structure makes your context clearest and most prominent.

Context Examples in Action

Let me show you how context transforms the same basic request across different scenarios:

Basic request: "Write an email about a project delay."

Scenario 1 - Internal team context: "I am a project manager writing to my engineering team about a two-week delay in our mobile app release. The delay is due to unforeseen technical challenges with the payment integration, not team performance issues. The team has been working hard and I want to keep morale high while being transparent about the situation. Write an email that explains the delay, acknowledges their efforts, and outlines our revised timeline."

Scenario 2 - Client context: "I am an account manager writing to a client about a two-week delay in their website launch. The delay is due to unforeseen technical challenges with third-party integrations. This client is understanding but has an internal marketing campaign timed to the launch. Write an email that takes responsibility, explains the situation professionally, presents a revised timeline, and offers a small accommodation to maintain goodwill."

Scenario 3 - Executive context: "I am a program director writing to our VP about a two-week delay in a strategic initiative she is tracking closely. The delay is due to resource constraints—two key team members were pulled to a more urgent project. I need to explain the delay, propose how to get back on track, and request a decision about resource allocation. Write an email that is concise, solution-focused, and frames the situation strategically."

Same basic situation (project delay), completely different emails based on context. Each addresses different concerns, uses different tone, and emphasizes different information.

Common Context Mistakes

After reviewing hundreds of prompts, I have noticed professionals consistently make certain context mistakes:

Mistake 1: Assuming shared knowledge

You know details about your industry, company, or situation that are not obvious to AI. Spell them out.

Mistake 2: Burying critical context

Important contextual details hidden in the middle of long paragraphs get missed. Lead with critical context or structure it prominently.

Mistake 3: Providing irrelevant context

Including background information that does not affect the output clutters your prompt and may confuse AI about what matters.

Mistake 4: Omitting stakeholder context

Failing to mention who will see, approve, or be affected by the output often results in wrong tone or emphasis.

Mistake 5: Forgetting constraint context

Not mentioning budget, time, resource, or policy constraints leads to suggestions you cannot implement.

Context Checklist

Before finalizing a prompt that requires context, check whether you have addressed:

□ **Who am I?** (Your role and authority) □ **What is my situation?** (Current circumstances) □ **Who is this for?** (Audience characteristics) □ **Why do I need this?** (Purpose and use case) □ **What constraints apply?** (Limitations and requirements) □ **What has happened before?** (Relevant history) □ **What industry factors matter?** (Domain-specific context)

Not every prompt needs all seven elements, but checking this list ensures you do not omit critical context.

When to Add vs. Withhold Context

Sometimes withholding certain context is strategic. If you want AI to generate creative ideas unconstrained by your assumptions, providing too much context can limit rather than enhance output.

For creative brainstorming, I often start without context: "Generate ten innovative ways to improve customer onboarding."

This produces a wide range of ideas, including some I never would have thought of because they do not fit my current constraints.

Then I take promising ideas and add context: "Take idea #3 (gamified onboarding) and adapt it for a B2B industrial equipment company with a six-month sales cycle and procurement teams as buyers."

This two-step approach gets creative breadth first, then practical adaptation.

But for most business tasks, more context is better. The risks of too little context (generic, unusable output) usually outweigh the risks of too much context (slightly constrained thinking).

Context Makes AI Your Partner

The fundamental shift that context enables is transforming AI from a generic tool into a partner that understands your specific situation.

Without context, you are asking a stranger for advice. The advice might be technically correct but not applicable to your circumstances.

With context, you are asking a well-informed colleague who understands your situation, your stakeholders, your constraints, and your goals. The advice becomes actionable.

This is why I always tell the business professionals I work with: "Spend an extra minute adding context. It will save you an hour of editing generic output into something useful."

Building Context-Rich Prompts

As you develop your prompting practice, develop the habit of asking yourself before each prompt: "What does AI need to know about my situation to give me useful output?"

This question will lead you to include the contextual details that transform generic responses into tailored solutions.

Context is not overhead. It is the mechanism that makes AI genuinely useful for your specific work.

In Chapter 5, we will explore another powerful technique for guiding AI output: providing examples. Where context describes your situation, examples show AI exactly what you want.

Chapter 5: Using Examples in Prompts: Learning by Demonstration

The Power of "Show, Don't Tell"

There is an old writing principle: show, don't tell. The same principle applies to prompt engineering. Sometimes the most effective way to communicate what you want is to show an example rather than describe it in words.

I discovered this while trying to generate email subject lines for a product launch. I spent twenty minutes describing the tone I wanted: "professional but intriguing, specific but not too detailed, benefit-focused but not salesy." The AI produced subject lines that were technically compliant with my description but still felt wrong.

Then I tried a different approach. I showed the AI three subject lines from previous successful campaigns and said, "Write new subject lines in this style." The results were immediately better. The AI understood in seconds what I had failed to communicate in twenty minutes of description.

Examples are extraordinarily efficient communication tools. They show AI the pattern you want without requiring you to articulate every characteristic of that pattern.

When Examples Work Best

Examples are particularly powerful in these situations:

Style matching: You want output that matches a specific style, tone, or voice that is difficult to describe in words.

Format replication: You need output in a specific structure or format.

Quality benchmarking: You want to show what "good" looks like for your purposes.

Pattern demonstration: You need AI to identify and replicate a pattern.

Tone calibration: You want a specific balance of characteristics (formal yet friendly, technical yet accessible) that is hard to specify verbally.

Not every prompt needs examples. For straightforward tasks with clear instructions, examples add unnecessary complexity. But when you find yourself writing long descriptions of what you want, consider whether an example would communicate more efficiently.

Types of Examples You Can Provide

Examples come in several forms, each useful for different purposes:

Input-output examples: Show AI both the input and desired output. This is powerful for transformation tasks.

Style examples: Show AI examples of the tone, voice, or format you want replicated.

Good vs. bad examples: Show AI both what you want and what you do not want, helping it understand the distinction.

Partial examples: Provide a template or partial example that AI should complete or adapt.

Multiple examples: Give several examples that demonstrate a pattern AI should recognize and apply.

Let's explore each type.

Input-Output Examples

Input-output examples show AI what you want it to do by demonstrating the transformation you desire.

This is especially powerful for tasks involving analysis, summarization, or transformation where describing the process is harder than showing it.

Example:

"Transform product features into customer benefits. Here are two examples:

Input: 256GB storage Output: Store over 50,000 photos and never worry about running out of space

Input: 12-hour battery life
Output: Work unplugged all day, from morning coffee to evening wrap-up

Now transform these features:

- Waterproof to 50 meters
- 5G connectivity
- Face recognition login"

The examples teach AI the pattern: take a technical spec, translate it into a practical user benefit, make it concrete and relatable. AI can now apply this pattern to new features.

I used this approach extensively while building ecommerce sites. Rather than describing how to write product benefits, I showed examples of good feature-to-benefit transformations. This produced consistently strong results across hundreds of products.

Style Examples

Style examples show AI the tone, voice, structure, or formatting you want replicated.

Example:

"Write three social media posts announcing our new office location. Match the style of these previous posts:

Example 1: 'Big news: We're growing! Our new headquarters opens next month at 123 Innovation Drive. Same great team, more space to serve you better. 🎉'

Example 2: 'Milestone alert: We just signed our 500th customer! Thank you for trusting us with your business. Here's to the next 500! 🚀'

Example 3: 'Behind the scenes: Ever wondered how we test our products? Take a virtual tour of our quality lab (link in bio). Spoiler: it's thorough! 🔬'

Now write three posts about our new office location."

These examples demonstrate:

- Length (short, tweet-sized)
- Structure (news + explanation + personal touch + emoji)
- Tone (excited but professional, customer-focused)
- Voice (we/our perspective, direct address to audience)

AI can now match these style characteristics without you describing each one explicitly.

Good vs. Bad Examples

Showing both good and bad examples helps AI understand subtle distinctions that are hard to describe verbally.

Example:

"Write a professional email declining a meeting request. Here is what NOT to do:

Bad example: 'Sorry, too busy. Maybe some other time.'

This is too abrupt and dismissive.

Here is what TO do:

Good example: 'Thank you for the invitation to discuss your proposal. Unfortunately, my schedule is fully committed through the end of the quarter. Would it be possible to reconnect in early April? I am genuinely interested in learning more about your work.'

This acknowledges the request, explains the situation, offers an alternative, and maintains the relationship.

Now write a professional decline for this situation: [your specific situation]"

The contrast between good and bad examples highlights what makes one approach effective and the other ineffective. AI learns not just what to do, but what to avoid.

Partial Examples (Templates)

Partial examples provide a structure that AI should complete or adapt. Think of these as templates with blanks to fill in.

Example:

"Write product comparison articles using this template:

[Product A] vs. [Product B]: Which [Product Category] Is Right for You?

Choosing between [Product A] and [Product B]? Both are excellent [product category], but they serve different needs. Here's what you need to know.

[Product A]: Best for [ideal use case]

- [Key strength 1]
- [Key strength 2]
- [Key strength 3]

[Product B]: Best for [ideal use case]

- [Key strength 1]
- [Key strength 2]
- [Key strength 3]

The Bottom Line: Choose [Product A] if [scenario]. Choose [Product B] if [scenario].

Now write a comparison article for our CRM Basic vs. CRM Pro plans."

The template shows AI the exact structure, flow, and elements you want. AI fills in the specific content while maintaining the proven format.

Multiple Examples to Show Patterns

When you provide multiple examples, AI can identify underlying patterns and apply them to new situations.

Example:

"Analyze these three customer complaints and identify the underlying issue:

Complaint 1: 'I've been waiting 20 minutes on hold. This is unacceptable.' Underlying issue: Long wait times for customer service

Complaint 2: 'Nobody seems to know the answer to my question. I've been transferred four times.' Underlying issue: Inadequate training or knowledge sharing among support staff

Complaint 3: 'I was told one thing by chat support and something completely different on the phone.' Underlying issue: Inconsistent information across support channels

Now analyze these new complaints and identify the underlying issues: [New complaints]"

Multiple examples teach AI the analysis pattern: look beyond the surface complaint to identify the root cause. This is more effective than describing the analysis process verbally.

How Many Examples to Provide

The right number of examples depends on complexity:

One example works when:

- The pattern is simple and clear
- You just need to establish format or style
- The task is straightforward

Two to three examples work when:

- You want to show a pattern across variations
- The desired approach has some nuance
- You want to demonstrate range within acceptable output

More than three examples work when:

- The pattern is complex or subtle
- You need to show multiple variations
- You are training AI to recognize categories or classifications

Diminishing returns set in after about five examples. If you need more than five examples to communicate your requirements, you probably need to reconsider your approach or break the task into smaller pieces.

Structuring Example-Enhanced Prompts

Examples should be integrated clearly into your prompt structure. I use this format:

1. **Task description**: What you want AI to do
2. **Example introduction**: Clear signal that examples follow
3. **Examples**: Labeled clearly (Example 1, Example 2, etc.)
4. **Application instruction**: Direct AI to apply the pattern

Full example:

"Write rejection emails for job candidates that are kind but clear.

Here are two examples of the style I want:

Example 1: 'Dear Sarah,

Thank you for taking the time to interview for the Marketing Manager position. We appreciated learning about your experience and approach.

After careful consideration, we have decided to move forward with a candidate whose background more closely aligns with our immediate needs. This was a difficult decision—your qualifications impressed us.

We will keep your information on file for future opportunities that may be a better fit. We wish you the best in your job search.

Best regards, [Name]'

Example 2: 'Dear Michael,

Thank you for your interest in the Software Engineer role and for speaking with our team.

We have decided to pursue candidates with more extensive experience in our specific tech stack. Your skills and background are strong; this decision reflects our particular needs rather than your qualifications.

We encourage you to apply for future openings that match your expertise more closely. Thank you again for your time and interest in our company.

Best regards, [Name]'

Now write a rejection email for [specific candidate and position]."

This structure makes it crystal clear what the examples are, what pattern they demonstrate, and what AI should do with that pattern.

Avoiding Example Pitfalls

Examples are powerful, but they can backfire if used incorrectly. Here are common mistakes:

Mistake 1: Inconsistent examples

Providing examples that do not actually follow the same pattern confuses AI about what you want.

Fix: Ensure your examples genuinely represent the pattern you want replicated.

Mistake 2: Unclear example boundaries

Failing to clearly mark where examples begin and end can cause AI to treat example content as instructions.

Fix: Use clear labels and structure: "Example 1:", "Example 2:", etc.

Mistake 3: Examples that are too similar

Providing multiple examples that are nearly identical does not help AI understand the pattern.

Fix: Choose examples that show variation within your desired pattern.

Mistake 4: Irrelevant examples

Including example elements that you do not actually want replicated.

Fix: Annotate examples to clarify which aspects should be replicated: "Match the tone and structure of this example, but use current product names and pricing."

Mistake 5: Overcomplicating with examples

Using examples when simple instructions would work better.

Fix: Reserve examples for situations where showing truly is more efficient than telling.

Examples for Different Task Types

Different types of tasks benefit from different example approaches:

For writing tasks: Style examples showing tone, voice, and structure

For analysis tasks: Input-output examples showing desired analytical approach

For formatting tasks: Template examples showing exact structure

For transformation tasks: Before-and-after examples showing desired changes

For classification tasks: Multiple examples of each category

For creative tasks: Multiple examples showing range of acceptable approaches

Matching your example type to your task type increases effectiveness.

Combining Examples with Context

Examples become even more powerful when combined with context. Context explains your situation; examples show what you want.

Example:

"I am writing quarterly update emails to investors in our early-stage startup. They want transparency but do not need excessive detail. Here is the style from our last quarterly update:

[Example of previous email]

Using this style, write an email about our Q3 results: revenue up 45%, three new enterprise customers, successful product launch, but also increased burn rate and delayed hiring plan."

Context (early-stage startup, investor audience, transparency priority) plus example (previous email style) gives AI everything needed to produce an appropriate email.

Building an Example Library

Just as I recommended building an instruction library in Chapter 3, I recommend building an example library for your common tasks.

Collect strong examples of:

- Emails you have written that achieved their purpose
- Documents that received positive feedback
- Marketing copy that performed well
- Analysis frameworks that worked
- Presentation structures that resonated

When you need AI to produce similar output, you can reference these proven examples rather than starting from scratch each time.

I maintain folders of effective examples organized by type: emails, proposals, presentations, social media posts, product descriptions. This library has saved me countless hours of re-explaining what I want.

When Not to Use Examples

While examples are powerful, they are not always appropriate:

Do not use examples when:

- Simple instructions would be clearer
- You want fresh approaches unconstrained by past patterns
- Examples would limit AI's creative range inappropriately
- The task is entirely different from anything you have done before

Examples are tools, not requirements. Use them when they enhance communication, skip them when they do not.

The Learning Principle

Examples work because they leverage how AI models learn. During training, AI learned patterns from millions of examples. When you provide examples in your prompt, you are giving AI a few-shot learning opportunity—teaching it a new pattern in real-time.

This is why examples often work better than detailed descriptions. You are working

Chapter 6: Prompting for Simple Tasks: One-Step Solutions

What Makes a Task Simple

A simple task is one that can be completed in a single step with a single output. There is no need for back-and-forth, no sequential dependencies, no complex decision trees. You ask, AI responds, and you have what you need.

Simple tasks are the foundation of practical AI use. They are the daily activities that, when done efficiently, save hours of time: drafting an email, summarizing a document, generating a list, answering a question, formatting data, creating a basic outline.

The mistake many professionals make is overcomplicating simple tasks. They add unnecessary complexity, hedge their requests, or fail to be direct about what they want. This turns a ten-second task into a frustrating five-minute exchange.

I have watched executives spend more time crafting prompts than the task itself would take if done manually. The art of simple task prompting is being clear, direct, and efficient.

The Anatomy of Simple Task Prompts

Effective simple task prompts have three elements:

Clear action verb: What should AI do?

Specific subject: What should it do this to?

Success criteria: How will you know it worked?

That is it. No elaborate context, no multiple examples, no complex conditions. Simple tasks deserve simple prompts.

Example of a simple task prompt: "Summarize this meeting transcript in five bullet points highlighting decisions made and action items assigned."

- Action verb: Summarize
- Subject: This meeting transcript
- Success criteria: Five bullet points, highlighting decisions and action items

This prompt will produce exactly what you need in seconds. No need for elaboration, context, or examples.

Common Simple Tasks in Business

Through my consulting work and my own experience building various businesses, I have identified the simple tasks that professionals perform most frequently:

Communication tasks:

- Draft standard emails (replies, confirmations, requests)
- Write brief announcements
- Create simple messages

Content tasks:

- Summarize documents or meetings
- Generate bullet point lists
- Create simple outlines
- Draft basic descriptions

Analysis tasks:

- Extract key points from text
- Identify main themes
- List pros and cons
- Highlight specific information

Formatting tasks:

- Convert formats (paragraph to bullets, etc.)
- Organize information
- Structure data
- Clean up formatting

Generation tasks:

- Create lists (ideas, questions, topics)
- Generate options or alternatives
- Produce variations on a theme
- Brainstorm basic concepts

Each category has its own best practices for prompting.

Communication Task Prompts

Communication tasks are among the most common simple tasks. The key is being specific about tone, length, and purpose.

Weak communication prompt: "Write an email."

This tells AI almost nothing. What kind of email? To whom? About what?

Strong communication prompts:

"Write a 3-sentence email to a client confirming our meeting tomorrow at 2pm and asking them to bring their Q3 sales data."

"Draft a brief Slack message to my team acknowledging their hard work this week and reminding them about Friday's deadline."

"Create a professional out-of-office message indicating I am unavailable until Monday and directing urgent matters to Jessica at jessica@company.com."

Each prompt specifies: format (email/message), recipient (client/team), content (what to communicate), and tone (professional/acknowledging).

Content Task Prompts

Content tasks transform existing material into different formats or lengths. Clarity about the transformation matters most.

Weak content prompt: "Make this shorter."

Shorter by how much? What should remain? What can be cut?

Strong content prompts:

"Reduce this 500-word article to exactly 150 words, preserving the three main recommendations and the supporting data for each."

"Convert this paragraph into a 5-item bullet point list, with each bullet being one complete sentence."

"Create a 3-sentence executive summary of this report focusing only on financial implications."

These prompts specify the desired length, format, and what content to prioritize.

Analysis Task Prompts

Analysis tasks ask AI to extract, identify, or evaluate information. Be specific about what type of analysis and what format for results.

Weak analysis prompt: "What do you think about this?"

AI's "thoughts" are not useful. You need specific analytical output.

Strong analysis prompts:

"Read this customer feedback and identify the top 3 complaints, listing each with a frequency estimate (how often it appears)."

"Review this proposal and list any claims that lack supporting data or evidence."

"Analyze this job description and extract the required skills, separating them into technical skills and soft skills."

These prompts specify what to analyze, what to look for, and how to present findings.

Formatting Task Prompts

Formatting tasks restructure information without changing content substantially. Precision about input format and desired output format is key.

Weak formatting prompt: "Organize this better."

"Better" is meaningless. Better how? According to what structure?

Strong formatting prompts:

"Convert this comma-separated list into a bulleted list with one item per line."

"Reorganize this information alphabetically by last name."

"Format this data as a simple table with three columns: Product, Price, Quantity."

These prompts make the transformation explicit and leave no room for interpretation.

Generation Task Prompts

Generation tasks create new content based on parameters you provide. These prompts need constraints to prevent overly broad or generic results.

Weak generation prompt: "Give me some ideas."

Ideas about what? How many? For what purpose?

Strong generation prompts:

"Generate 5 potential titles for a blog post about time management for remote workers. Each title should be 6-10 words."

"List 10 questions a prospective customer might ask about our pricing model."

"Brainstorm 8 possible names for a project management app focused on creative teams. Names should be memorable, easy to spell, and suggestive of collaboration."

These prompts specify quantity, topic, purpose, and constraints.

The Importance of Constraints in Simple Tasks

Constraints are even more important for simple tasks than for complex ones because they prevent scope creep. Without constraints, a simple task can balloon into something unnecessarily elaborate.

Key constraints for simple tasks:

Length constraints: "In 3 sentences," "Exactly 5 bullet points," "Under 100 words"

Scope constraints: "Focus only on financial impacts," "Include only the top 3," "Address only the implementation phase"

Format constraints: "As a numbered list," "In a single paragraph," "As a table"

Time constraints: "For the next quarter," "Since January," "Over the past year"

These constraints keep simple tasks simple.

When Simple Prompts Fail

Even simple task prompts sometimes fail. The most common reasons:

Failure reason 1: Ambiguous action verb

"Handle this" or "Deal with this" are not clear actions. Use specific verbs: summarize, list, convert, extract, generate.

Failure reason 2: Vague success criteria

Without clear success criteria, you get output that is technically responsive but not actually useful.

Fix: Add specific measurable criteria. Not "make it shorter" but "reduce to 150 words."

Failure reason 3: Missing key information

Even simple tasks need relevant information. If you ask AI to "draft a reply," AI needs to know: reply to what? Saying what?

Fix: Include or reference the necessary information.

Failure reason 4: Asking for multiple things

Trying to accomplish several tasks in one prompt often results in AI doing none of them well.

Fix: Separate into distinct prompts or explicitly number the tasks.

Efficiency Patterns for Repeated Simple Tasks

For simple tasks you perform repeatedly, create templated prompts that you can quickly adapt.

I maintain templates like:

Email reply template: "Draft a [tone] email reply to [recipient] [action needed]. Keep it under [X] sentences."

Summary template: "Summarize this [document type] in [X] bullet points focusing on [specific aspect]."

List generation template: "Generate [X number] [item type] for [purpose]. Each should [constraint]."

When a simple task comes up, I fill in the bracketed elements rather than writing a prompt from scratch.

This saves time and ensures consistency. My summaries are always structured the same way. My email drafts always hit the right tone. My lists always meet my quality standards.

The One-Minute Rule

I have a personal rule for simple task prompts: if crafting the prompt takes more than one minute, I am overcomplicating it.

Simple tasks should have simple prompts. If you find yourself writing multiple paragraphs of context and examples for a straightforward task, step back and simplify.

Ask yourself: "What is the absolute minimum information AI needs to complete this task successfully?"

Often, it is much less than you think.

Quality Control for Simple Tasks

Because simple tasks are fast, it is tempting to skip quality control. This is a mistake. Always review AI output before using it, even for simple tasks.

Quick quality checks:

Did it follow your instructions? Length, format, scope all correct?

Is it accurate? If summarizing or extracting, is the information correct?

Is the tone appropriate? Professional when needed, friendly when appropriate?

Does it accomplish your goal? Not just technically correct but actually useful?

These checks take seconds but prevent embarrassing mistakes.

Building Simple Task Competency

Mastering simple task prompting is about developing habits:

Habit 1: Lead with the action verb. Always start with what you want AI to do.

Habit 2: Be specific about quantity. "Some ideas" becomes "5 ideas." "A brief summary" becomes "a 3-sentence summary."

Habit 3: Include format requirements. Specify bullets vs. paragraphs, table vs. list, etc.

Habit 4: Add one key constraint. Length, scope, focus, or tone—pick the constraint that matters most.

Habit 5: Review before using. Quick check for accuracy and appropriateness.

These habits make simple task prompting automatic. You will find yourself drafting effective prompts without conscious thought.

The Compound Effect of Simple Tasks

Individual simple tasks save minutes. But professionals perform dozens of simple tasks daily. Those minutes compound into hours.

Consider a typical day:

- Draft 8 emails: 40 minutes saved
- Summarize 3 meeting notes: 30 minutes saved
- Create 2 simple lists: 10 minutes saved
- Format 4 documents: 20 minutes saved

That is nearly two hours of reclaimed time, simply by efficiently prompting for simple tasks.

Multiply that across a team of 20 people, and you have 40 hours of gained productivity daily. Across a company of 200, that is 400 hours. The impact is enormous.

This is why simple task prompting matters. Not because any individual task is critical, but because the accumulated efficiency transforms how work gets done.

Simple Does Not Mean Simplistic

Simple task prompting is not about dumbing things down. It is about clarity and efficiency. A well-crafted simple task prompt demonstrates sophistication in its precision.

Compare: "Write something about the new policy" (simplistic and useless)

"Draft a 4-sentence email to department heads announcing the new travel policy, emphasizing that it takes effect November 1 and includes a link to full details" (simple but sophisticated)

The second prompt is concise yet complete. It communicates exactly what is needed without unnecessary elaboration.

When to Escalate from Simple to Complex

Sometimes what seems like a simple task is actually complex. Indicators that you need a more complex approach:

- Your simple prompt fails repeatedly
- The task requires multiple steps or decision points
- Context significantly affects the outcome
- The task needs examples to clarify expectations
- Multiple stakeholders have different requirements

When you hit these indicators, move to the complex task techniques covered in Chapter 7.

But often, the issue is not that the task is complex—it is that your prompt lacks specificity. Before escalating to complex prompting, ensure your simple prompt includes clear action verb, specific subject, and measurable success criteria.

Simple Task Mastery

Simple task prompting is a leverage point. Mastering it does not require learning complex frameworks or advanced techniques. It requires discipline: be clear, be specific, be concise.

The professionals who gain the most from AI are often not those tackling the most complex problems. They are those who efficiently handle dozens of simple tasks daily, freeing their time and mental energy for work that cannot be automated.

In Chapter 7, we turn to the other end of the spectrum: complex tasks that require multi-step approaches, careful sequencing, and sophisticated prompting strategies.

Chapter 7: Prompting for Complex Tasks: Mastering Multi-Step Requests

Understanding Task Complexity

A complex task is one that requires multiple steps, conditional logic, or substantial judgment to complete. Unlike simple tasks that can be handled in one prompt-response exchange, complex tasks need structure, sequencing, and often iteration.

I learned the hard way that treating complex tasks like simple tasks leads to frustration. Early in my work with AI agents, I would ask for complete strategic analyses in single prompts. The results were always disappointing—too shallow, missing key considerations, or focused on the wrong aspects.

The breakthrough came when I started breaking complex tasks into clear sequential steps, with each step building on the previous one. Suddenly, AI could handle sophisticated work that previously seemed beyond its capabilities.

The key insight: AI is better at following a well-defined process than at inventing one. Your job is to provide that process.

Identifying Complex Tasks

How do you know when a task is complex enough to require multi-step prompting?

Indicators of complexity:

Multiple objectives: The task requires achieving several different goals, not just one.

Sequential dependencies: Later steps depend on results from earlier steps.

Judgment required: The task involves evaluation, assessment, or subjective decision-making.

Substantial research: The task requires processing significant information before generating output.

Multiple stakeholders: Different audiences or perspectives need to be considered.

High stakes: The output will inform important decisions or be seen by critical stakeholders.

If your task has two or more of these indicators, use a multi-step approach.

The Sequential Prompting Method

The most effective approach for complex tasks is sequential prompting: breaking the task into discrete steps and prompting for each step separately.

The basic structure:

Step 1 - Information gathering: Collect, analyze, or process necessary information.

Step 2 - Framework development: Create structure, identify key elements, or establish approach.

Step 3 - Content generation: Produce the main output based on previous steps.

Step 4 - Refinement: Review, critique, and improve the output.

Let me demonstrate with a real example from my consulting work.

Complex task: Develop a content marketing strategy for a B2B software company.

Sequential approach:

Prompt 1 (Information gathering): "Based on this company description, identify 5 key customer pain points that our software addresses and list 3 main competitor approaches to content marketing in this space."

Review the response. This gives you the foundation for strategic thinking.

Prompt 2 (Framework development): "Given these customer pain points and competitor approaches, propose 3 distinct content strategy directions we could pursue, each with a brief rationale for why it could be effective."

Review the response. This gives you strategic options to evaluate.

Prompt 3 (Content generation): "Take Strategy Direction 2 (thought leadership positioning). Develop it into a detailed 6-month content plan including content types, topics, channels, and success metrics. Present it as a structured plan with clear sections."

Review the response. This gives you a detailed, implementable plan.

Prompt 4 (Refinement): "Review this content plan and identify any gaps, unrealistic elements, or areas that need more detail. Provide specific recommendations for improvement."

This creates a much stronger final output than trying to get everything in one prompt.

The Iterative Refinement Pattern

For complex tasks where the initial output needs substantial improvement, use iterative refinement: generate, critique, refine, repeat.

Pattern structure:

Iteration 1: "Generate [output] with [basic requirements]."

Iteration 2: "Review this output and identify the weakest elements. What is missing? What could be stronger?"

Iteration 3: "Improve the output by addressing the issues you identified. Specifically strengthen [weak areas noted in iteration 2]."

Iteration 4 (if needed): Continue refining specific aspects until output meets your standards.

I used this pattern extensively while writing my books. Rather than trying to get perfect content in one pass, I would generate, critique, and refine repeatedly. This iterative approach produced much better results than attempting perfection immediately.

The Structured Analysis Pattern

For tasks requiring deep analysis, use this pattern:

Step 1 - Data review: "Review [data/document/information] and extract the 10 most significant facts, trends, or patterns."

Step 2 - Pattern identification: "Analyze these facts and identify 3-4 underlying patterns or themes that connect them."

Step 3 - Implication analysis: "For each pattern identified, explain what it means for [specific context] and what actions it suggests."

Step 4 - Recommendation synthesis: "Based on this analysis, provide 3 prioritized recommendations with clear rationale."

This pattern ensures thorough, structured thinking rather than superficial analysis.

The Debate Pattern for Decision-Making

For complex decisions, have AI argue multiple sides:

Step 1 - Position development: "Present the strongest possible case for [Option A], including supporting evidence and addressing potential counterarguments."

Step 2 - Counter-position: "Now present the strongest possible case against [Option A], including what we might be overlooking or underestimating."

Step 3 - Alternative evaluation: "Present the case for [Option B] as an alternative."

Step 4 - Synthesis: "Based on these arguments, what are the key decision factors we should weigh? What additional information would strengthen our decision confidence?"

This pattern prevents confirmation bias and ensures consideration of multiple perspectives.

I use this pattern when making significant business decisions. Having AI argue both sides helps me identify blind spots in my thinking.

The Expert Panel Pattern

For complex problems requiring diverse expertise, simulate multiple expert perspectives:

Prompt structure: "Analyze [problem] from three expert perspectives:

1. A [Expert Type 1] would focus on [their domain]. What would they identify as key considerations?
2. A [Expert Type 2] would emphasize [their domain]. What would they flag as critical?
3. A [Expert Type 3] would prioritize [their domain]. What would they recommend?

After presenting all three perspectives, identify where they agree and where they conflict. What does this tell us about the problem?"

Example: "Analyze our customer retention problem from three expert perspectives:

1. A data analyst would focus on the numbers. What patterns would they identify?
2. A customer experience designer would emphasize the user journey. What friction points would they flag?
3. A business strategist would prioritize competitive positioning. What strategic factors would they highlight?

Present all three perspectives, then synthesize insights."

This pattern provides multidimensional analysis without needing multiple actual experts.

Managing Complex Task Scope

Complex tasks can spiral out of control. Manage scope by:

Setting boundaries upfront: "Focus only on [specific aspect]. Exclude [out-of-scope elements]."

Defining completion criteria: "The analysis is complete when we have [specific deliverables]."

Limiting depth: "Provide high-level analysis with 2-3 supporting points for each area, not exhaustive detail."

Constraining time or resources: "Recommend approaches implementable within [constraints]."

These boundaries keep complex tasks manageable.

The Documentation Pattern

For tasks producing important outputs, document your reasoning:

Step 1: Generate the main output.

Step 2: "Explain the reasoning behind the three most important choices or recommendations in this output. What alternatives did you consider? Why was this approach selected?"

This documentation helps you evaluate quality and helps others understand the thinking behind recommendations.

Breaking Down Multi-Layered Tasks

Some complex tasks have multiple layers that need to be addressed in sequence.

Example: Developing a new pricing strategy

Layer 1 - Market analysis: Understand competitive landscape and customer willingness to pay.

Layer 2 - Cost analysis: Determine minimum viable pricing based on costs and margin requirements.

Layer 3 - Value analysis: Identify how customers value different features or service levels.

Layer 4 - Strategy development: Design pricing structure that reflects value while remaining competitive.

Layer 5 - Implementation planning: Determine how to introduce new pricing and manage existing customers.

Each layer becomes a separate prompting sequence. Trying to address all five layers in one prompt produces superficial results.

The Validation Pattern

For high-stakes complex tasks, add validation steps:

After main output: "Review this [output] as a critical evaluator. What assumptions might be wrong? What have we not considered? Where is the reasoning weakest?"

Then: "Based on these critiques, what specific changes would strengthen this work?"

This pattern catches errors and gaps before they become problems.

Handling Conditional Logic

Complex tasks often involve "if-then" logic. Structure these conditions clearly:

Pattern: "Analyze [situation]. If [condition A] applies, recommend [approach X]. If [condition B] applies instead, recommend [approach Y]. If neither condition applies, recommend [approach Z]. Explain which condition applies in our case and provide the corresponding recommendation."

This ensures AI considers contingencies appropriately.

The Synthesis Pattern

When working with multiple sources or perspectives, synthesize explicitly:

After gathering multiple inputs: "I have received three different analyses of [problem]: [Source 1 findings], [Source 2 findings], [Source 3 findings]. Synthesize these into a unified understanding. Where do they agree? Where do they conflict? What explains the conflicts? What integrated conclusion can we draw?"

Synthesis transforms multiple fragments into coherent understanding.

Managing Long Complex Processes

For very complex tasks with many steps, create a master framework first:

Meta-prompt: "I need to [complex task objective]. Break this into 6-8 major steps that would need to be completed in sequence. For each step, briefly describe what would be accomplished."

Review the framework. Adjust as needed.

Then prompt for each step: "Let's complete Step 1: [description]. [Specific requirements for this step]."

This top-down approach ensures your process is logical before you invest time in execution.

Quality Control for Complex Tasks

Complex task outputs require careful review:

Completeness check: Did AI address all required elements?

Logic check: Does the reasoning make sense? Are conclusions supported?

Consistency check: Do different parts of the output align or contradict each other?

Feasibility check: Are recommendations actually implementable?

Audience check: Is this appropriate for the intended stakeholders?

Create a checklist for your common complex tasks so you review consistently.

When to Use Human Judgment

AI is a tool for complex tasks, not a replacement for human judgment. Reserve human involvement for:

Strategic decisions: Final choices with significant business impact.

Subjective assessments: Evaluations requiring deep contextual understanding.

Stakeholder management: Navigating organizational dynamics.

Creative direction: Setting overall vision and direction.

Risk evaluation: Assessing acceptable risk levels.

Use AI to inform these judgments, not make them.

The Learning Curve for Complex Prompting

Complex task prompting takes practice. Your first attempts will be inefficient. You will discover missing steps, unclear instructions, or logical gaps.

This is normal. Each complex task you prompt teaches you about:

- How to break down complexity
- What level of detail different steps need
- Where AI struggles and needs more guidance
- How to sequence steps effectively

Keep notes on what works. Build templates for your common complex tasks. Your efficiency will improve dramatically with practice.

Complex Tasks as AI's Strength

Paradoxically, complex tasks are where AI adds the most value—when properly prompted. AI never gets tired, never loses focus, and can hold large amounts of information in consideration simultaneously.

A human analyst might lose track after considering five factors. AI can juggle fifteen factors without confusion. A human writer might struggle to maintain consistency across a long document. AI maintains consistency naturally.

The key is providing structure. AI plus human process design equals capabilities neither possesses alone.

Moving to Specialized Applications

This chapter covered general approaches to complex tasks. The next two chapters explore specialized applications: creative prompting (Chapter 8) and technical prompting (Chapter 9), where we adapt these foundational techniques to specific domains.

Chapter 8: Debugging Prompt Problems: Fixing What Goes Wrong

The Inevitability of Failed Prompts

Every prompt engineer, from beginner to expert, writes prompts that fail. The response is wrong, incomplete, off-target, or simply useless. This is not a sign of incompetence. It is the nature of communicating with AI.

I have written thousands of prompts. Many failed on first attempt. The difference between frustration and progress is understanding why prompts fail and how to fix them systematically.

This chapter is about developing a debugging mindset: treating failed prompts not as dead ends but as diagnostic information that tells you how to improve.

The Four Categories of Prompt Failure

Prompt failures fall into four categories, each requiring different solutions:

Comprehension failures: AI misunderstands what you want.

Execution failures: AI understands but cannot execute properly.

Quality failures: AI produces output but it does not meet your standards.

Scope failures: AI does too much or too little.

Identifying which category your failure falls into points you toward the right fix.

Comprehension Failures

Symptom: The AI response is completely off-topic or addresses something you did not ask for.

Causes:

- Ambiguous phrasing
- Unclear referents (what "it" or "this" refers to)
- Buried requests hidden in rambling text
- Conflicting instructions

Example of comprehension failure:

Prompt: "Can you help me with that thing we discussed about the marketing campaign? Make it better but keep it similar to what we usually do."

AI response: Provides generic marketing advice completely unrelated to your specific needs.

Why it failed: "That thing" is undefined. "Make it better" is vague. "What we usually do" assumes shared context that does not exist.

How to fix:

Debugged prompt: "Review this email draft for our product launch campaign. Improve clarity and strengthen the call to action while maintaining our professional but friendly tone. Keep the length under 200 words."

What changed:

- Specific subject: "this email draft"
- Clear action: "improve clarity and strengthen call to action"
- Defined constraints: tone, length
- No ambiguous references

Debugging process for comprehension failures:

Step 1: Identify what AI misunderstood. Did it address the wrong topic? Wrong format? Wrong audience?

Step 2: Find the ambiguity. What word or phrase could be interpreted multiple ways?

Step 3: Add specificity. Replace vague language with precise terms.

Step 4: Remove pronouns. Replace "it," "this," "that" with specific nouns.

Step 5: Test again.

Execution Failures

Symptom: AI understands what you want but cannot produce it properly. The attempt is in the right direction but inadequately executed.

Causes:

- Insufficient information provided
- Task too complex for single prompt
- Conflicting requirements
- Missing examples or context

Example of execution failure:

Prompt: "Write a proposal for implementing AI tools across our company."

AI response: Produces a generic proposal that does not address your specific company context, industry, current state, or stakeholder concerns.

Why it failed: Not enough information. AI cannot write a company-specific proposal without company-specific details.

How to fix:

Debugged prompt: "Write a proposal for implementing AI writing tools (specifically for email, reports, and documentation) at our 150-person professional services firm. Our employees currently resist new technology, so emphasize ease of use and time savings. The proposal will be reviewed by partners who care most about billable hour impact and client quality. Include implementation timeline, budget estimate, and success metrics."

What changed:

- Specific tools and use cases
- Company context (size, industry, culture)
- Stakeholder information (concerns, priorities)
- Required sections

Debugging process for execution failures:

Step 1: Identify what is missing. What information would you need if you were doing this task?

Step 2: Add necessary context. Provide background, constraints, stakeholder information.

Step 3: Break complex tasks into steps. If the task is too big for one prompt, use sequential prompting.

Step 4: Provide examples if needed. Show what good output looks like.

Step 5: Test again.

Quality Failures

Symptom: AI produces output in the right format and on the right topic, but the quality is inadequate. It is generic, shallow, or not useful.

Causes:

- No quality criteria specified
- Missing examples of desired quality
- Insufficient constraints
- No specificity about depth or detail

Example of quality failure:

Prompt: "Analyze this customer feedback data."

AI response: Provides superficial analysis: "Customers mentioned pricing frequently. Service quality was also discussed. Some customers were satisfied while others were not."

Why it failed: No quality criteria. What does "analyze" mean? What depth? What format? What insights?

How to fix:

Debugged prompt: "Analyze this customer feedback data and produce a structured report with three sections: 1) Top 5 themes ranked by frequency with percentage of mentions, 2) Representative quotes for each theme, 3) Specific actionable recommendations for each theme. For recommendations, prioritize quick wins that address the most frequent complaints."

What changed:

- Defined analysis structure
- Specified output format
- Required quantification (frequency, percentages)
- Demanded specificity (representative quotes, actionable recommendations)
- Added prioritization criteria

Debugging process for quality failures:

Step 1: Define what "quality" means for this specific output. What characteristics distinguish good from mediocre?

Step 2: Add quality criteria to your prompt. Be explicit about depth, detail, specificity.

Step 3: Provide examples of desired quality level if available.

Step 4: Add constraints that force higher quality (e.g., "include data to support each claim").

Step 5: Test again.

Scope Failures

Symptom: AI does too much (produces overly elaborate output) or too little (output is insufficiently detailed).

Causes:

- No scope boundaries specified
- Unclear about what to include/exclude
- Missing length or detail requirements

Example of scope failure (too much):

Prompt: "Explain how to use our project management software."

AI response: Produces a 2000-word comprehensive manual covering every feature in exhaustive detail.

Why it failed: No scope limits. AI interpreted "explain how to use" as "explain everything."

How to fix:

Debugged prompt: "Write a 300-word quick start guide for new users of our project management software. Cover only the 3 most essential functions: creating projects, assigning tasks, and tracking progress. Assume users are not technical and need simple step-by-step instructions."

What changed:

- Length limit (300 words)
- Scope limit (3 essential functions only)

- Detail level (simple, step-by-step)
- Audience context (not technical)

Example of scope failure (too little):

Prompt: "Give me ideas for improving employee engagement."

AI response: Lists 3 generic ideas without detail or context.

Why it failed: No indication of how much depth or how many ideas needed.

How to fix:

Debugged prompt: "Generate 8 specific, actionable ideas for improving employee engagement at a remote-first tech company with 75 employees. For each idea, include: 1) What to do, 2) Why it works, 3) Approximate cost/effort to implement. Prioritize low-cost, high-impact options."

What changed:

- Specified quantity (8 ideas)
- Required detail level (what, why, cost for each)
- Added context (remote-first, tech, company size)
- Added prioritization criteria

Debugging process for scope failures:

Step 1: Identify whether you got too much or too little.

Step 2: Add scope boundaries: length limits, specific sections required, inclusion/exclusion criteria.

Step 3: Specify level of detail needed for each element.

Step 4: Test again.

The Systematic Debugging Method

When a prompt fails, follow this systematic process:

1. Categorize the failure Which category: comprehension, execution, quality, or scope?

2. Identify the specific problem What exactly is wrong? Be precise.

3. Hypothesize the cause Why did this happen? What was missing or unclear?

4. Make one targeted change Fix the specific issue you identified. Change only one thing.

5. Test the revised prompt Did it improve? If yes, continue. If no, try a different fix.

6. Iterate as needed Repeat until output meets your requirements.

Chapter 9: Creative Prompting: Unleashing Your Imagination

The Creative Challenge

Creative prompting is fundamentally different from the instructional and analytical prompting we have covered so far. When asking AI to write a report or analyze data, there are clear success criteria: accuracy, completeness, clarity. When asking AI to generate creative content, success is more subjective: Is it original? Compelling? On-brand? Emotionally resonant?

I learned this distinction while creating marketing content for my ecommerce sites. My early attempts at creative prompting used the same direct, constrained approach that worked for analytical tasks. The results were technically correct but creatively flat. The headlines were grammatical but not attention-grabbing. The product descriptions were accurate but not compelling.

Creative prompting requires a different approach: less constraint, more inspiration; less specification, more exploration; less perfection, more iteration.

The Creative Prompt Mindset

Creative prompting is not just about writing clever instructions — it's about thinking differently. To craft truly imaginative AI responses, you need to adopt a creative mindset built on flexibility, experimentation, and patience.

1. Think in quantity before quality.
Start by generating many ideas. Don't aim for perfection in the first try — let your imagination explore freely. Once you have several options, you can refine and select the strongest ones.

2. Embrace iteration.
Your first creative prompt is rarely the final masterpiece. Expect to adjust, test, and rework your ideas. Iteration is not failure — it's how creativity evolves.

3. Use constraints to fuel creativity.
Boundaries often spark innovation. Having limits (like word count, tone, or format) forces you to think more resourcefully. Constraints give structure to imagination.

4. Learn from examples — don't copy them.
Examples can guide your direction, but they shouldn't box you in. Let them serve as inspiration for originality, not imitation.

5. Accept imperfection.
Every creative output is a draft — a foundation for something greater. Treat it as raw material to polish and perfect later.

Developing this mindset changes everything. When you expect instant perfection, frustration follows. But when you expect to sculpt rough ideas into something brilliant, you'll unlock the real potential of creative prompting.

Types of Creative Tasks

Creative prompting can take many forms, each requiring a slightly different approach. The main categories include:

- **Concept Generation:** Brainstorming new ideas, product names, taglines, or themes.
- **Narrative Creation:** Crafting stories, scenarios, or case studies that illustrate a message or emotion.
- **Persuasive Writing:** Designing marketing copy, calls to action, or attention-grabbing headlines.
- **Descriptive Writing:** Painting vivid scenes or describing products, people, or events.
- **Stylistic Adaptation:** Rewriting existing material in different tones, voices, or writing styles.

Each type of creative work benefits from its own prompting strategies — and we'll look at these in more detail next.

Concept Generation Prompts

When your goal is to generate ideas, focus on **divergence first** — explore as many directions as possible before narrowing them down.

A weak prompt might sound like:

"Give me an idea for a marketing campaign."

That usually produces a single, generic answer. Instead, think expansively — ask the AI to explore multiple themes, styles, or audiences.

Concept Generation Prompts

To generate strong ideas, your prompts should encourage exploration rather than narrow thinking. The goal is to produce a wide variety of possibilities before selecting the most promising ones.

Weak Prompt Example:

"Give me an idea for a marketing campaign."

This kind of request usually results in one vague or uninspired idea.

Stronger Prompt Example:

"List ten creative marketing campaign ideas for a new eco-friendly clothing brand. Include at least one social media challenge, one influencer idea, and one community event."

By adding structure, constraints, and variety, you guide the AI to think broadly while maintaining focus.

Tip: When brainstorming, use action verbs like *list, explore, compare,* or *invent*. These encourage the AI to produce more ideas, not just one.

Narrative Creation Prompts

Narrative prompts are used to build stories, examples, or case studies that engage readers emotionally or intellectually.

Weak Prompt Example:

"Write a story about artificial intelligence."

Stronger Prompt Example:

"Write a 200-word short story about an artist who uses an AI tool to rediscover her creativity. Include a twist ending that shows how technology reshapes her view of art."

Adding specific characters, emotions, and goals helps the AI create a more meaningful and cohesive narrative.

Tip: Specify tone (e.g., hopeful, suspenseful, humorous) and length to help shape the storytelling style.

Persuasive Writing Prompts

Persuasive prompts are ideal for marketing, advertising, or motivational writing. The goal is to inspire action or belief.

Weak Prompt Example:

"Write an ad for a new phone."

Stronger Prompt Example:

"Write a 3-sentence ad for a new AI-powered phone targeting college students. Highlight speed, smart features, and affordability. End with a catchy slogan."

Tip: Define the target audience and call to action clearly — this helps the AI tailor the message to the right emotional triggers.

Descriptive Writing Prompts

Descriptive prompts bring scenes, products, or emotions to life. They rely on sensory details and vivid imagery.

Weak Prompt Example:

"Describe a garden."

Stronger Prompt Example:

"Describe a hidden garden at sunrise, filled with dew-covered flowers, the sound of sparrows, and the scent of jasmine."

The more sensory cues you include, the more dynamic and immersive the AI's description becomes.

Tip: Use prompts that invite the five senses — sight, sound, touch, taste, and smell — to create vivid realism.

Stylistic Adaptation Prompts

Stylistic prompts help the AI rewrite existing content in different tones, voices, or writing styles.

Weak Prompt Example:

"Rewrite this in another style."

Stronger Prompt Example:

"Rewrite this paragraph in the style of a motivational speaker addressing young entrepreneurs. Use short, energetic sentences and uplifting language."

Tip: Mention the specific style, audience, and emotional tone you want. You can even reference a famous writer, speaker, or genre for inspiration.

Summary

Creative prompting is an art of exploration. It's not about finding a single perfect answer — it's about discovering possibilities and shaping them through iteration. By adjusting tone, context, and structure, you can guide AI to produce results that are not only imaginative but also aligned with your vision.

Prompting Strategies for Each Creative Task

Now that we've covered the main categories of creative work, let's look at practical strategies for designing and improving prompts in each. The goal is to combine structure with imagination so that every prompt leads to richer and more purposeful results.

1. Concept Generation Strategies

Concept generation is all about **divergent thinking** — exploring as many ideas as possible before narrowing down the best. To make this process effective:

- **Start broad:** Ask for multiple directions, perspectives, or themes.
  Example: "Give me ten ideas for an educational app that helps children learn math through games, songs, or storytelling."
- **Add creative angles:** Include unexpected twists or constraints to make the ideas stand out.
  Example: "Brainstorm five product ideas that combine sustainability with fashion technology."
- **Refine and rank:** After you get a list, follow up with prompts like:
  "Rank these ideas by originality and market potential."
- **Iterate intentionally:** Keep prompting until one idea feels complete enough to develop further.

Key Tip: Don't stop after one round. Great ideas emerge through continuous prompting, reviewing, and improving.

2. Narrative Creation Strategies

Narrative prompts help shape stories, scripts, or illustrative examples. Here's how to strengthen them:

- **Set a clear goal:** Define what you want the story to communicate (emotion, lesson, or message).
  Example: "Write a short story that teaches teamwork through the perspective of two competing AI robots."
- **Specify structure:** Ask for parts such as *introduction, conflict, climax, and resolution.*
  Example: "Create a 3-part story about a student learning to trust AI tools during an art competition."
- **Add character details:** The more personality you include, the more vivid the story becomes.
- **Guide tone and style:** Use adjectives like *humorous, suspenseful,* or *inspirational* to fine-tune the voice.

Key Tip: Great storytelling prompts balance emotion and logic — they ask the AI to *show* meaning through actions, not just *tell* it directly.

3. Persuasive Writing Strategies

When writing to persuade — for marketing, speeches, or motivational messages — clarity and audience awareness are essential.

- **Define your audience:** Who are you trying to reach? (e.g., parents, students, entrepreneurs)
- **Clarify your purpose:** What action should readers take? (e.g., subscribe, donate, buy)
- **Use emotional hooks:** Add words that create curiosity, urgency, or excitement.
- **Request multiple formats:** Ask the AI to provide options — like short taglines, full paragraphs, or bullet versions.

Example Prompt:

"Write three short promotional paragraphs for a new online course on AI literacy. Make one sound motivational, one friendly, and one professional."

Key Tip: Compare the results and merge the best ideas into a polished final draft.

4. Descriptive Writing Strategies

Descriptive writing should transport the reader into a scene or experience. To achieve this effect:

- **Anchor the setting:** Define the *where* and *when* clearly.
- **Engage all senses:** Ask the AI to include what can be seen, heard, touched, or felt.
- **Use metaphors or analogies:** Encourage imaginative comparisons to strengthen visuals.
- **Add emotion:** Link sensory details to feelings — calm, excitement, nostalgia, etc.

Example Prompt:

"Describe a futuristic classroom filled with holographic teachers and AI learning companions. Include how students feel walking into the room for the first time."

Key Tip: Descriptive prompts thrive on vivid specificity. The more details you feed the model, the more lifelike the output becomes.

5. Stylistic Adaptation Strategies

When adapting a style, tone, or voice, the key is to **define both the source and the target styles.**

- **Identify the tone:** (e.g., formal, conversational, poetic, technical)
- **Specify the audience:** (e.g., middle school students, business professionals, artists)

- **Provide examples:** Give one or two short excerpts that represent the desired voice.
- **Request comparison:** Ask the AI to explain how the new style differs from the original.

Example Prompt:

"Rewrite this paragraph in the tone of a TED Talk speaker. Add enthusiasm, simplify jargon, and end with an inspiring takeaway."

Key Tip: Style-based prompting is powerful for brand consistency and educational tone control. Always refine based on rhythm, vocabulary, and readability.

Conclusion

Mastering creative prompting is a process of *asking better questions*. The more precisely you define what you want — tone, format, emotion, or perspective — the closer the AI moves toward your vision. Every creative task becomes easier when guided by structure, context, and curiosity.

The Creative Constraints Paradox

Paradoxically, adding creative constraints often produces better results than complete freedom.

Useful creative constraints:

Format constraints: "Write in haiku form," "Create six-word stories," "Use only questions"

Limitation constraints: "Without using these overused words: [list]," "Without directly naming the product"

Perspective constraints: "From the viewpoint of the product itself," "As if explaining to a child," "As a skeptic being convinced"

Style constraints: "In the style of a film noir detective," "As a scientific paper," "Like a motivational speech"

These constraints force creative problem-solving rather than default patterns.

Example:

"Write product headlines for our task management app using these constraints:

- Each headline must be exactly 6 words
- Cannot use these overused words: easy, simple, amazing, revolutionary, best
- Must include a concrete benefit

- Should create curiosity

Generate 10 options."

The constraints push AI toward originality.

The Variation Technique

For creative work, generate variations and select the best:

The theme variation approach:

"Write 5 variations of the same marketing message, each with a different theme:

1. Urgency theme (time-sensitive, act now)
2. Social proof theme (others are using this)
3. Transformation theme (before and after)
4. Exclusivity theme (limited, special access)
5. Problem-solving theme (we solve your pain point)

Message to vary: Our AI writing tool helps businesses create content faster. Each variation: 2 sentences, under 30 words total."

The tone variation approach:

"Write the same announcement in five different tones:

1. Professional and formal
2. Casual and friendly
3. Enthusiastic and energetic
4. Minimalist and understated
5. Playful and humorous

Announcement: We're launching a new feature that lets teams collaborate in real-time. Each version: 3 sentences."

Variations let you evaluate different creative directions before committing to one.

The Elaboration Technique

Start with a seed and ask AI to elaborate creatively:

Seed to story:

"Take this one-line concept: 'A small business owner discovers our software by accident and it changes everything.'

Develop this into a 200-word story that:

- Shows the accident/discovery naturally
- Makes the transformation specific and believable
- Feels authentic, not like an ad
- Includes real challenges they faced
- Ends with a subtle insight, not a hard sell"

Seed to campaign:

"Take this positioning: 'The project management tool for teams who hate project management tools.'

Develop this into a full campaign concept including:

- Why this positioning resonates
- Three headline variations
- Core messages to emphasize
- Visual/design direction ideas
- Sample social media posts
- How to prove this claim

Present as a structured campaign brief."

Elaboration prompts transform sparks into fully developed creative work.

The Remix Technique

Combine elements in new ways to create originality:

"I want to create a unique employee onboarding experience. Remix concepts from these three domains:

1. Video game design: progression systems, achievements, tutorials
2. Theater: storytelling, character development, immersive experiences
3. Fine dining: curation, pacing, memorable moments

Generate 5 onboarding concepts that creatively combine elements from at least two of these domains. For each, explain: the core concept, which domains you're remixing, why this would be memorable, and how it would work practically."

Remixing forces creative connections between unrelated concepts.

Quality Evaluation for Creative Work

Evaluating creative output is inherently subjective, but you can apply criteria:

Originality: Does it feel fresh or formulaic?

Relevance: Does it connect to your brand, audience, and goals?

Clarity: Is the core message clear despite creative flourishes?

Memorability: Would this stick with someone after a single exposure?

Actionability: Does it inspire the desired response?

Brand alignment: Does it sound like your brand?

Use these criteria consistently across creative options to make selection less arbitrary.

The Refinement Cycle for Creative Work

Creative prompting rarely produces final work in one pass. Expect refinement:

Cycle 1 - Generate: Create multiple options with variety.

Cycle 2 - Select: Choose the strongest 2-3 options.

Cycle 3 - Refine: "Take option 2 and strengthen [specific aspect]."

Cycle 4 - Polish: "Review this and improve word choice, rhythm, and impact."

Each cycle improves quality while preserving creative direction.

I use this cycle for all marketing content. Generate 10 concepts, select 3, develop those 3 fully, refine the best one, polish until it shines.

Maintaining Creative Authenticity

AI-generated creative work can sound generic if not carefully directed. Maintain authenticity by:

Providing genuine examples: Show real brand voice, not aspirational generic examples.

Including real details: Specific product features, actual customer pain points, true differentiators.

Avoiding clichés: Explicitly tell AI to avoid overused phrases.

Adding human touches: Edit AI output to include specific details only you know.

Testing with real audiences: Does it resonate or fall flat?

The best creative work combines AI's generative capacity with your authentic brand knowledge.

Creative Prompting as Collaboration

Think of creative prompting as collaborating with a creative partner who has infinite energy but needs direction. You provide:

- Strategic direction (what we're trying to achieve)
- Brand knowledge (how we sound, what we value)
- Audience insight (what resonates with our people)
- Quality standards (what's good enough)

AI provides:

- Volume of options
- Variation and diversity
- Freedom from creative blocks
- Fresh perspectives

Together, you produce creative work neither could achieve alone.

Moving to Technical Applications

This chapter explored creative prompting where originality and impact matter most. Chapter 10 shifts to the opposite end of the spectrum: technical prompting for coding, data analysis, and other precision-required tasks where accuracy trumps creativity.

Chapter 10: Technical Prompting: Coding and Data with AI

The Precision Requirement

Technical prompting differs from creative prompting in a fundamental way: precision matters absolutely. A marketing headline that is 90% right might still be effective. Code that is 90% right does not work.

My background in development taught me that technical work requires exactness. When I started using AI for coding tasks, I initially applied the same flexible, iterative approach I used for creative work. This failed repeatedly. Code would almost work, have subtle bugs, or make incorrect assumptions about data structures.

Technical prompting requires a different approach: explicit requirements, clear specifications, thorough testing, and systematic debugging.

Types of Technical Tasks

Technical tasks that benefit from AI assistance include:

Code generation: Writing functions, scripts, or programs

Code explanation: Understanding existing code

Debugging: Finding and fixing errors

Code transformation: Converting between languages or refactoring

Data analysis: Processing and analyzing datasets

Query writing: SQL, database queries, API calls

Documentation: Writing technical documentation

Algorithm design: Developing logical approaches to problems

Each requires specific prompting strategies.

Code Generation Prompts

When generating code, provide complete specifications:

Weak code generation prompt: "Write a function to validate email addresses."

This lacks critical details: What language? What validation rules? How should errors be handled?

Strong code generation prompt:

"Write a Python function that validates email addresses according to these requirements:

Function name: validate_email Parameter: email_string (string) Return: Boolean (True if valid, False if invalid)

Validation rules:

- Must contain exactly one @ symbol
- Must have at least one character before @
- Domain must have at least one dot
- Domain must have at least 2 characters after the final dot
- No spaces allowed anywhere
- Accept letters, numbers, dots, hyphens, and underscores

Include docstring explaining function purpose and parameters. Include at least 3 inline comments explaining key logic.

Also provide 5 test cases (3 valid, 2 invalid) with expected results."

This prompt specifies:

- Language (Python)
- Function signature
- Exact validation rules
- Documentation requirements
- Test cases

The resulting code will be precise and usable.

The Specification Pattern for Code

For any code generation, provide:

1. Language and version "In Python 3.9" or "In JavaScript ES6"

2. Input specifications What data comes in? What format? What types?

3. Output specifications What should be returned? What format? What type?

4. Logic requirements What rules? What calculations? What conditions?

5. Error handling What could go wrong? How should errors be handled?

6. Edge cases What unusual inputs should be handled?

7. Constraints Performance requirements? Dependencies allowed? Style guidelines?

More specification yields better code.

Code Explanation Prompts

When asking AI to explain code, direct attention to what matters:

Weak code explanation prompt: "Explain this code."

This produces generic line-by-line description.

Strong code explanation prompts:

"Explain this JavaScript function focusing on:

1. What problem it solves (high-level purpose)
2. The algorithm or approach it uses
3. Any non-obvious logic that might confuse readers
4. Potential edge cases or limitations
5. Whether this is an efficient approach or if there are better alternatives

[code here]

Write the explanation for mid-level developers who understand JavaScript but might not recognize this specific pattern."

This targets the explanation to your needs.

For learning purposes:

"I'm learning Python and don't understand this code:

[code here]

Explain it in three layers:

1. Plain English: What does this accomplish in simple terms?
2. Step-by-step: What happens at each major step?
3. Technical details: What Python concepts or patterns is this using?

Assume I understand basic programming but not Python-specific syntax."

Layered explanation supports learning progressively.

Debugging Prompts

When asking AI to debug, provide context about the problem:

Weak debugging prompt: "This code doesn't work."

What does "doesn't work" mean? What error? What expected behavior?

Strong debugging prompt:

"This Python function is supposed to calculate the average of numbers in a list, but it's producing incorrect results.

[code here]

Problem symptoms:

- Input: [10, 20, 30] → Output: 15 (Expected: 20)
- Input: [5, 5, 5] → Output: 5 (Correct)
- Input: [100, 200] → Output: 100 (Expected: 150)

I suspect the issue is in the calculation logic, possibly with integer division.

Please:

1. Identify the bug
2. Explain why it causes these specific symptoms
3. Provide the corrected code
4. Suggest how to test that the fix works"

This gives AI everything needed: the code, expected vs. actual behavior, your hypothesis, and what you need from the fix.

Code Transformation Prompts

When converting or refactoring code:

For language conversion:

"Convert this Python function to JavaScript, maintaining the exact same logic and behavior:

[Python code]

Requirements:

- Use modern JavaScript (ES6+)
- Preserve all comments, updating language-specific references
- Use equivalent JavaScript data structures
- Include brief notes on any significant differences in how Python vs JavaScript handles this logic"

For refactoring:

"Refactor this JavaScript code to improve readability and maintainability:

[code]

Goals:

- Extract repeated logic into helper functions
- Add descriptive variable names (avoid single letters except for standard loops)
- Add JSDoc comments for functions
- Ensure each function does one thing well
- Maintain exact same functionality and behavior

Explain the key changes you made and why they improve the code."

Specify goals so AI knows what "better" means.

Data Analysis Prompts

When analyzing data with AI:

Weak data analysis prompt: "Analyze this data."

Generic analysis produces generic insights.

Strong data analysis prompt:

"Analyze this sales data CSV to answer these specific questions:

1. What are the top 5 products by revenue?
2. Which month had the highest sales growth compared to the previous month?
3. Are there any seasonal patterns (quarterly or monthly)?
4. Which sales region is underperforming relative to others?
5. Are there any products with declining sales trends?

For each question:

- Provide the specific answer
- Show the relevant data/calculations
- Explain what this means for business decisions

Data is in this format:

- Columns: Date, Product, Region, Units_Sold, Revenue
- Date format: YYYY-MM-DD
- 2000 rows covering 2 years

Present findings as a structured report with sections for each question."

This directs analysis toward actionable insights.

SQL and Query Prompts

For database queries:

Weak query prompt: "Write a SQL query to get customer data."

Vague about schema, what customer data, and what conditions.

Strong query prompt:

"Write a SQL query for PostgreSQL 13 with these requirements:

Schema:

- customers table: id, name, email, signup_date, account_type
- orders table: id, customer_id, order_date, total_amount, status

Requirements:

- Find all customers who signed up in 2024
- Who have account_type = 'premium'
- And have placed at least 3 orders with status = 'completed'
- Return: customer name, email, signup date, total order count, sum of order amounts
- Order results by total order amount (highest first)
- Limit to top 50 customers

Include comments explaining each major part of the query. Make it efficient (avoid nested queries if possible)."

Provides schema, exact requirements, and desired output format.

Algorithm Design Prompts

For logical problem-solving:

"I need an algorithm to match freelancers to projects based on skills and availability.

Context:

- 100 freelancers with skill sets (arrays of skills)
- 20 open projects with required skills
- Each freelancer has availability (hours/week)
- Each project has time requirements (hours)
- Multiple freelancers can work on one project if needed

Goals:

- Maximize the number of projects that get adequately staffed
- Prefer exact skill matches over partial matches
- Consider freelancer availability constraints

Provide:

1. High-level algorithm approach (conceptual steps)
2. Pseudocode showing the logic
3. Key data structures to use
4. Potential issues or edge cases to consider
5. Estimated complexity (Big O)

Don't write full code yet—I want to review the approach first."

Start with algorithm design before implementation to ensure sound approach.

Documentation Prompts

For technical documentation:

"Write API documentation for this function:

[code]

Documentation should include:

- Brief description (one sentence, what it does)
- Detailed explanation (when to use it, how it works)
- Parameters table (name, type, required/optional, description)
- Return value (type and description)
- Example usage (2-3 practical examples with realistic inputs)
- Error conditions (what errors can occur and why)
- Related functions or alternatives

Format as Markdown. Write for developers who are new to our codebase."

Specify documentation structure and audience.

The Testing Mindset

Always request tests alongside code:

"Along with the function, provide:

1. Unit tests covering normal cases
2. Tests for edge cases
3. Tests for error conditions
4. Brief explanation of what each test validates"

Tests ensure code works and help you understand intended behavior.

Handling Technical Constraints

Technical work often has specific constraints:

Performance constraints: "The function must process 10,000 records in under 1 second."

Dependency constraints: "Use only Python standard library, no external packages."

Compatibility constraints: "Must work on both Python 3.8 and 3.11."

Style constraints: "Follow PEP 8 style guidelines strictly."

Security constraints: "Input must be sanitized to prevent SQL injection."

Include these explicitly in prompts.

The Iterative Technical Process

Even with precise prompts, technical work often requires iteration:

Iteration 1: Generate initial code based on specifications.

Iteration 2: Test the code. Identify issues.

Iteration 3: "This code produces [wrong output] for [input]. The issue seems to be [hypothesis]. Fix this while maintaining all other functionality."

Iteration 4: Test again. Refine as needed.

Technical iteration should be systematic, testing-driven, and hypothesis-based.

Common Technical Prompt Mistakes

Mistake 1: Insufficient specifications

Assuming AI knows standard approaches for your domain. Be explicit.

Mistake 2: No test cases

Not providing or requesting test cases to validate correctness.

Mistake 3: Ignoring edge cases

Focusing only on the happy path, not error conditions.

Mistake 4: Wrong abstraction level

Asking for too much or too little in one prompt. Break complex systems into functions or modules.

Mistake 5: Unclear data structures

Not specifying exactly how data is structured.

Combining Technical and Business Context

The best technical prompts combine precise specs with business context:

"Write a Python function to calculate customer lifetime value (CLV).

Business context:

- We're a SaaS company with monthly subscriptions
- Average customer stays 18 months

- We want to predict future value to prioritize sales efforts

Technical requirements: [detailed function specs]

The calculation should be simple enough that non-technical business users can understand the logic when we explain it to them."

Business context helps AI make appropriate technical trade-offs.

When to Use Technical Prompting

Use AI for technical tasks when:

- You need boilerplate or standard patterns quickly
- You're learning and need explanations
- You're debugging and need fresh perspectives
- You're working in an unfamiliar language or framework
- You need documentation written
- You're prototyping and speed matters more than optimization

Don't rely solely on AI for:

- Mission-critical production# What to Say When I Talk to AI: Prompt Engineering Guide

Chapter 11: Building Your Personal AI Toolkit

Reusable Prompts, Templates, and Frameworks That Accelerate Your Work

Now that you've explored the science and psychology behind effective prompting, it's time to create something that truly belongs to you — a personal **AI toolkit**. Think of this as your digital toolbox filled with **prompts, templates, and frameworks** that will save you hours of time, enhance your productivity, and give your conversations with AI consistency and power.

Just as writers have notebooks and artists have sketchbooks, AI users need a library of **go-to prompts** — reusable structures that can adapt to any project, profession, or creative goal. Once you start building and refining your own toolkit, you'll notice that prompting becomes not just a task, but a habit — a structured way of thinking that sharpens clarity, focus, and results.

1. Why You Need a Personal Prompt Library

Each time you talk to AI, you're not just typing words — you're programming intent. When you reuse successful prompts, you begin to recognize what works and why. Over time, you'll develop a collection that fits your voice, goals, and workflow.

Having your own toolkit allows you to:

- Work faster with tested templates.
- Maintain consistent tone and quality.
- Create repeatable results for writing, teaching, research, or design.
- Train your AI assistant to understand your preferences and patterns.

2. Building Reusable Prompts

Start by saving your best-performing prompts. Group them into categories such as:

- **Creative Writing Prompts** – for storytelling, book outlines, and marketing copy.
- **Business Prompts** – for emails, reports, or strategy planning.
- **Teaching Prompts** – for lessons, examples, and classroom materials.
- **Technical Prompts** – for code, debugging, or AI framework development.

Each prompt should be written in a way that's **modular** — meaning you can replace keywords, topics, or goals without rewriting the entire structure.

Example Template:

"Act as a [role] and help me [goal]. Provide [number] detailed examples in [tone/style]. Include [specific elements or steps]."

This one line can serve hundreds of uses — from writing an article to designing a course or developing a chatbot flow.

3. Using Prompt Frameworks

Frameworks are guiding structures that help you build better instructions. They give your prompts shape and logic.

Common Prompt Frameworks:

- **RACE** – Role, Action, Context, Expectation.
- **SPEC** – Situation, Purpose, Example, Clarity.
- **TAPE** – Task, Audience, Parameters, End Goal.

By following a framework, you make your AI think methodically. The clearer the structure, the stronger the output.

4. Templates for Everyday Use

Below are examples you can personalize and store in your toolkit:

🧠 Thinking Prompt

"Think step-by-step before answering. Explain your reasoning clearly, as if teaching a beginner."

📝 Writing Prompt

"Act as an editor. Rewrite this paragraph for clarity, conciseness, and emotional impact."

💡 Creative Prompt

"Generate 5 original ideas for a social media post about [topic] that will inspire and educate."

📈 Strategy Prompt

"Act as a business advisor. Create a 7-day plan to increase engagement for [project or product]."

You can keep these in a digital notebook or use a spreadsheet to label them by category, goal, and tone.

5. Maintaining and Expanding Your Toolkit

Your AI toolkit is never finished — it grows as you do. Every great output you receive can be refined and added back to your collection. Over time, you'll have your own personalized **Prompt Portfolio** — a set of reusable tools that reflect your expertise.

To maintain it:

- **Review weekly:** Add, edit, or test new prompts.
- **Refine tone:** Adjust for personality and consistency.
- **Save your winners:** Keep copies of high-quality responses for future reference.

6. The Future of Your Toolkit

Your personal toolkit isn't just for convenience — it's your bridge to mastery. It transforms AI from a helper into a creative partner. Whether you're writing books, teaching classes, coding software, or running a business, your reusable prompts become a signature part of your workflow.

Each template is a small piece of wisdom — built once, used forever.
And the more you add to your collection, the more powerful your relationship with AI becomes.

In Summary

A personal AI toolkit is your long-term advantage.
It saves time, enhances creativity, and teaches you to think like a designer of conversations.
Build it, refine it, and let it grow with you — one reusable prompt at a time.

Chapter 12: The Future of Prompting

Preparing for the Evolution of AI and the Next Era of Human–Machine Collaboration

The journey of learning how to talk to AI doesn't end here—it's only the beginning. Artificial Intelligence is evolving faster than any technology in history, and the skills you've built through this book will continue to grow in value as AI becomes more capable, more conversational, and more integrated into everyday life.

Prompting will change—but **your ability to think clearly, question creatively, and communicate precisely** will always remain the foundation of this new digital language.

1. The Changing Role of the Human in AI Conversations

At first, prompting seemed like typing commands into a computer.
But over time, it has become a collaboration—a partnership between human intention and machine intelligence.

Future systems will require less instruction and more insight.
They'll learn your tone, understand your goals, and even anticipate your next question.
Yet the human role will never disappear—it will simply **shift from instructing to guiding**, from requesting answers to shaping direction.

💡 *Tomorrow's best AI users won't just know what to ask. They'll know how to teach AI what matters.*

2. The Evolution of Prompt Engineering

Prompt engineering will grow beyond single lines of text. It's already expanding into **multimodal prompting**, where you can guide AI with images, voice, video, and emotion.

Soon, your "prompt" might be a combination of:

- **A picture you upload** for visual analysis.
- **A tone of voice** that conveys urgency or calm.
- **A gesture or command** that starts a process in real time.

AI will not just respond to *what you say*, but *how you say it.*
Understanding this shift means learning to design experiences, not just prompts.

3. The Age of Personalized AI

In the coming years, every person will have their own **AI companion or assistant**, built to understand their values, voice, and goals.
Your prompting style will become a kind of personal fingerprint—a reflection of how you think, solve problems, and express creativity.

You may train your AI on your past writing, your projects, or even your personality traits. Over time, it will begin to mirror your reasoning patterns, offering advice that feels distinctly *you.*

💡 *The better you understand how to guide AI, the more personal—and powerful—your assistant becomes.*

4. New Tools, Same Principles

While technologies, platforms, and models will continue to change, the principles you've learned remain constant:

1. **Clarity** — Define what you want clearly.
2. **Context** — Give the AI enough background to respond intelligently.
3. **Creativity** — Ask in new ways to unlock unexpected insights.
4. **Control** — Direct the style, tone, and depth of responses.

Master these four, and you'll adapt easily to any future system, regardless of the tool's name or interface.

5. Ethics and Responsibility in the Next Era

As AI becomes more powerful, your influence as a user grows.
Every prompt you create contributes to shaping how these systems behave.
That's why **ethical prompting**—rooted in fairness, privacy, and respect—will define the future of human–AI collaboration.

The next generation of prompt engineers won't just be technologists; they'll be *designers of trust.*
They'll ensure AI serves humanity's best interests by promoting truth, transparency, and compassion in every interaction.

💡 *Prompt engineering is no longer just about output—it's about impact.*

6. Continuous Learning and Adaptation

Staying relevant means staying curious.
Keep experimenting with new models, studying their differences, and observing how subtle changes in phrasing affect responses.

Save what works. Share what surprises you. Document what fails.
Every discovery strengthens your intuition and helps you lead in this constantly changing field.

You're not just a user—you're an **AI communicator** shaping how technology understands the human voice.

7. Your Journey Ahead

The next evolution of prompting will belong to those who treat it as both art and science.
Where others see instructions, you'll see conversation.
Where others see code, you'll see creativity.

You now carry a toolkit of frameworks, templates, and strategies that will grow alongside you.
As AI transforms workplaces, classrooms, and communities, your skill in speaking its language will make you a translator between innovation and understanding.

The more clearly you communicate with AI, the more meaningfully AI will communicate with the world.

So keep refining your voice.
Keep exploring what's possible.
And most of all—keep talking to AI like it's a partner in progress.

In Summary

Chapter 12 isn't an ending—it's an invitation.
The world is entering a new era where human creativity and artificial intelligence will shape each other in ways we're only beginning to imagine.
Your prompts are the bridge between the two.

Write wisely. Experiment boldly.
Because the conversation you start today will help define the language of tomorrow.

🔤 AI Glossary — Letter A

Algorithm

A step-by-step set of instructions that tells a computer how to solve a problem or perform a task. In AI, algorithms are the "recipes" that guide machines in recognizing patterns, learning from data, and making predictions.

Artificial Intelligence (AI)

The science of creating machines that can perform tasks that normally require human intelligence — such as understanding language, recognizing images, solving problems, or making decisions.

Artificial Neural Network (ANN)

A system inspired by how the human brain works, made up of layers of connected nodes (neurons). Each node processes information and passes it along, allowing the system to "learn" patterns from data.

Artificial General Intelligence (AGI)

A theoretical form of AI that would be able to understand, learn, and perform any intellectual task a human can do. AGI doesn't exist yet, but it represents the ultimate goal of AI research — true human-like intelligence.

Artificial Narrow Intelligence (ANI)

AI designed for a specific task, such as language translation, facial recognition, or driving a car. Most AI today is narrow — powerful at one thing, but unable to perform unrelated tasks.

Activation Function

A key part of neural networks that decides whether a neuron should be "activated" or not. It helps the network handle complex patterns, turning raw numbers into meaningful signals during learning.

Anomaly Detection

A technique used in AI to find unusual patterns or behaviors that don't fit expected data. It's commonly used in fraud detection, cybersecurity, and system monitoring to identify potential problems.

Attention Mechanism

A method used in advanced AI models (like transformers) that allows the system to focus on the most relevant parts of the input. It helps the AI "pay attention" to important words or data points when generating responses.

Augmented Intelligence

AI systems designed not to replace humans, but to assist them. Augmented intelligence emphasizes collaboration — combining human creativity and judgment with machine speed and accuracy.

Autonomous System

A system that can operate, make decisions, or take actions without direct human control. Examples include self-driving cars, delivery drones, or robotic assistants that use AI to navigate and respond to their environment.

🔠 AI Glossary — Letter B

Backpropagation

A key learning process used in neural networks to adjust the model's internal settings (weights) based on the errors it makes. By "propagating" mistakes backward through the network, the AI learns to improve accuracy over time.

Bayesian Network

A graphical model that represents the relationships between variables and their probabilities. It helps AI systems reason under uncertainty — for example, predicting the likelihood of an event based on known factors.

Bias in AI

When an AI system produces unfair or unbalanced results due to biased data or flawed training methods. Bias can affect hiring systems, loan approvals, and facial recognition — making fairness testing essential in AI development.

Big Data

Extremely large and complex datasets that traditional computers can't easily process. AI tools use big data to learn patterns, make predictions, and uncover insights across industries like healthcare, finance, and marketing.

Binary Classification

A machine learning task where the AI must choose between two possible outcomes — such as "spam or not spam," "yes or no," or "disease or no disease." It's one of the most basic types of AI decision-making.

Bit

The smallest unit of digital data, representing a value of **0** or **1**. In AI and computing, bits form the foundation for all data processing, storage, and communication. Eight bits make up one **byte**, and together they represent everything from numbers and text to images and videos.

Bitwise Operation

A type of mathematical operation that works directly on the binary representation (bits) of data. Bitwise operators (such as AND, OR, XOR, and NOT) are used in AI programming to control low-level logic, optimize performance, and manipulate data efficiently.

Blockchain AI

The combination of blockchain (a secure, distributed ledger) and artificial intelligence to improve transparency, data security, and trust in AI-driven systems.

Bot

Short for "robot," a bot is a program that performs automated tasks. In AI, chatbots are designed to simulate human conversation, while other bots perform repetitive digital actions like data scraping or scheduling.

Brute Force Algorithm

A simple but computationally expensive problem-solving method that tries every possible solution until it finds the correct one. Though inefficient, it guarantees accuracy for small problems.

Batch Learning

A method where an AI model is trained on a complete dataset all at once, rather than learning continuously. It's efficient for large, static datasets but less adaptable to changing data over time.

Behavioral Analytics

AI techniques that analyze user actions, preferences, or digital patterns to predict future behavior. Often used in marketing, fraud detection, and personalized recommendations.

🔠 AI Glossary — Letter C

Chatbot

An AI-powered program designed to simulate human conversation through text or voice. Chatbots can answer questions, provide customer support, teach lessons, or help automate business communication using natural language processing.

Classification

A core machine learning task where AI assigns input data into specific categories or labels — such as identifying whether an email is "spam" or "not spam." Classification models are trained using labeled examples to recognize patterns.

Clustering

An unsupervised learning technique where AI groups similar pieces of data together based on shared characteristics. Unlike classification, clustering doesn't use labeled data — it helps uncover hidden patterns or natural groupings within datasets.

Cognitive Computing

A branch of AI that mimics human reasoning, perception, and decision-making. Cognitive systems analyze unstructured data, recognize language and emotions, and provide intelligent suggestions — much like how the human brain interprets information.

Computer Vision

A field of AI that enables machines to "see" and interpret visual information such as images or videos. Computer vision powers facial recognition, object detection, medical imaging, and autonomous vehicles.

Convolutional Neural Network (CNN)

A specialized type of neural network used primarily for image and video analysis. CNNs automatically detect visual features like edges, shapes, and textures, allowing machines to recognize objects or patterns with high accuracy.

Context Window

The range of text or tokens that a language model can "see" and use at one time to generate its response. A larger context window allows AI to remember more of the conversation, leading to better understanding and consistency.

Corpus

A large and structured collection of texts used to train or evaluate language models. In AI, a corpus provides the examples that teach the model how words and phrases are used in real-world contexts.

Cross-Validation

A model evaluation technique used in machine learning to test how well a model generalizes to new, unseen data. The dataset is divided into parts (folds), and the model is trained and tested multiple times to ensure accuracy and reliability.

Cybernetics

The interdisciplinary study of communication and control in both machines and living organisms. In AI, cybernetics explores feedback loops — how systems monitor and adjust their behavior to maintain balance and achieve goals.

🔠 AI Glossary — Letter D

Data Analytics

The process of examining, cleaning, and interpreting data to uncover useful information and patterns. In AI, data analytics helps models learn from real-world data to make predictions and informed decisions.

Data Labeling

The act of tagging or annotating raw data with meaningful labels — such as identifying images with "cat" or "dog." Labeled data is essential for training supervised machine learning models.

Data Mining

The practice of exploring large datasets to discover hidden patterns, trends, or relationships. AI-powered data mining helps businesses predict customer behavior, detect fraud, and improve decision-making.

Data Science

An interdisciplinary field that combines statistics, programming, and AI to extract insights from data. Data scientists build predictive models, analyze trends, and guide data-driven decisions.

Dataset

A structured collection of data used to train or test AI models. A dataset can include text, images, numbers, or audio. The quality and diversity of the dataset directly affect how well an AI performs.

Decision Tree

A visual and logical model used in AI for decision-making. Each branch represents a question or condition, and each leaf represents an outcome. Decision trees are popular for their simplicity and interpretability.

Deep Learning

A subset of machine learning that uses multi-layered neural networks to learn complex patterns. Deep learning powers technologies like voice recognition, autonomous driving, and image generation.

Dimensionality Reduction

A mathematical process used to simplify datasets by reducing the number of variables while preserving important information. It helps AI models work faster and more efficiently, especially with large data.

Domain Adaptation

A technique in AI that allows a model trained on one dataset to perform well on a different but related dataset. It helps AI generalize better to new environments or data types.

Drift Detection

The process of identifying when an AI model's performance declines because real-world data has changed. Detecting data drift ensures the model stays accurate and up-to-date over time.

AI Glossary — Letter E

Edge AI

Artificial Intelligence that runs directly on local devices (like smartphones, cameras, or IoT sensors) instead of relying on cloud servers. Edge AI allows faster responses, improved privacy, and reduced internet dependency.

E-Learning AI

The use of AI in online education to personalize learning experiences, analyze student performance, and recommend tailored study materials. E-Learning AI helps teachers and learners adapt lessons to individual needs.

E-commerce AI

AI applications that enhance online shopping experiences. These systems recommend products, predict customer behavior, optimize pricing, and improve inventory management for e-commerce platforms.

E-mail Filtering AI

AI systems that automatically detect and organize incoming emails — such as sorting spam, prioritizing important messages, or detecting phishing threats — using natural language and pattern recognition.

E-Transaction Security

AI-based systems that monitor and protect online financial transactions. They detect unusual activity, verify identities, and prevent fraud in digital banking and online payment systems.

E-book Recommendation Systems

AI algorithms that suggest books or reading materials based on user preferences, past selections, or browsing behavior. They enhance reading platforms by delivering personalized content to readers.

E-Brainstorming

The use of AI tools to assist with creative idea generation. E-brainstorming platforms help individuals and teams generate fresh perspectives, organize thoughts, and develop new solutions quickly.

Embedding

A mathematical representation of data (like words, sentences, or images) in numerical form. In AI, embeddings help models understand meaning, context, and similarity — crucial for natural language processing and image recognition.

Emotion AI

Also called Affective Computing, it's a branch of AI that recognizes, interprets, and responds to human emotions using facial expressions, voice tones, or physiological signals. It's used in customer service, education, and healthcare.

Ensemble Learning

A technique that combines multiple AI models to produce stronger, more accurate results than a single model could achieve alone. Common ensemble methods include bagging, boosting, and stacking.

🔤 AI Glossary — Letter F

1. Face Recognition AI

A technology that uses machine learning and computer vision to identify or verify a person's identity based on facial features. It's used in security systems, smartphones, and law enforcement, but also raises privacy and ethical concerns.

Federated Learning

A training method that allows multiple devices or organizations to collaboratively train an AI model without sharing raw data. Each participant trains the model locally, and only updates are shared — improving data privacy and security.

Feature Extraction

The process of identifying the most important characteristics or variables from raw data. In AI, feature extraction helps reduce complexity and improve model accuracy by focusing on relevant information.

Fine-Tuning

A process of retraining a pre-trained AI model on a smaller, specific dataset to make it more accurate for a particular task. Fine-tuning allows developers to customize general-purpose models for specialized applications.

Forecasting Model

An AI system that predicts future events or trends based on historical data. Forecasting models are widely used in business, weather prediction, finance, and supply chain management.

Fuzzy Logic

An AI reasoning system that allows for partial truths rather than strict "true or false" decisions. It's useful for handling uncertainty in real-world situations like temperature control, medical diagnosis, and robotics.

Feature Engineering

The process of creating, transforming, or selecting data features to improve machine learning model performance. It's a key step that combines human insight with data science techniques to optimize accuracy.

False Positive

A situation in which an AI system incorrectly identifies something as true when it's not. For example, a spam filter marking a legitimate email as spam. Reducing false positives improves reliability and user trust.

False Negative

The opposite of a false positive — when an AI system fails to identify something that is true. For example, a medical AI missing signs of a disease. Balancing false positives and negatives is vital in sensitive applications.

Feature Map

In deep learning, particularly in convolutional neural networks (CNNs), a feature map represents visual patterns detected in an image. It helps the network recognize shapes, textures, and other important details.

AI Glossary — Letter G

GAN (Generative Adversarial Network)

A type of deep learning model with two neural networks — a **generator** and a **discriminator** — that work against each other. The generator creates data (like images or text), while the discriminator evaluates it for authenticity. This competition helps the model generate highly realistic outputs such as AI-generated art or photos.

General AI (Artificial General Intelligence)

A theoretical form of AI capable of understanding, learning, and applying knowledge across multiple domains — much like a human being. Unlike narrow AI, General AI could perform any intellectual task without specific training.

Genetic Algorithm

An optimization technique inspired by natural selection. It uses processes like mutation, crossover, and selection to evolve solutions to complex problems — often used in robotics, scheduling, and engineering design.

Geospatial AI

The combination of artificial intelligence with geographic data (maps, satellite images, or GPS data) to analyze spatial patterns. It's used in urban planning, agriculture, environmental monitoring, and disaster management.

Gesture Recognition

A branch of computer vision that interprets human movements — such as hand waves or facial expressions — as commands. It's commonly used in gaming, virtual reality, and touchless interfaces.

GPT (Generative Pre-trained Transformer)

A family of large language models developed by OpenAI. GPT models are trained on vast text datasets and can generate human-like text, write essays, code, or answer questions — forming the foundation for conversational AI systems like ChatGPT.

Gradient Descent

An optimization algorithm used in training neural networks. It minimizes the model's prediction error by gradually adjusting weights in the direction of the steepest decrease in loss — similar to rolling downhill to find the lowest point.

Graph Neural Network (GNN)

A type of neural network designed to process data structured as graphs — with nodes (points) and edges (connections). GNNs are used in recommendation systems, molecule analysis, and social network modeling.

Ground Truth

The real, verified data used to measure how accurate an AI model's predictions are. For example, in image recognition, the "ground truth" is the actual label of what the image shows. It's essential for evaluating model performance.

Guided Learning

An AI-assisted educational approach that provides learners with personalized hints, explanations, and progress tracking. Guided learning uses data analytics and adaptive models to support student growth in real time.

🔤 AI Glossary — Letter H

Hallucination (in AI)

A phenomenon where an AI model generates information that appears confident and factual but is actually incorrect or fabricated. Hallucinations occur when the model fills gaps in knowledge or misinterprets data. Managing them requires clear prompts, human review, and fact-checking.

Heuristic Algorithm

A problem-solving method that uses experience-based shortcuts to find good — though not always perfect — solutions quickly. Heuristic algorithms are common in AI search systems, decision-making, and optimization problems where speed matters more than precision.

Hidden Layer

A layer of neurons in a neural network that processes inputs between the input and output layers. Hidden layers extract complex patterns from data and enable the network to make accurate predictions or classifications.

Human-Computer Interaction (HCI)

The study and design of how people interact with computers and AI systems. HCI focuses on usability, accessibility, and user experience, ensuring that AI tools feel intuitive and supportive to human users.

Human-in-the-Loop (HITL)

An AI training or decision process that includes active human participation. Humans review, correct, or guide the AI's outputs to ensure quality, fairness, and ethical alignment — especially important in high-stakes fields like healthcare and law.

Hybrid AI

An approach that combines two or more types of AI — such as symbolic reasoning (rule-based) and machine learning (data-driven) — to create systems that are both interpretable and powerful. Hybrid AI blends logic with learning for smarter, explainable outcomes.

Hyperparameter

A setting or configuration that controls how an AI model learns, such as learning rate, batch size, or number of layers. Unlike model parameters learned automatically, hyperparameters are manually chosen to optimize training performance.

Hyperparameter Tuning

The process of finding the best hyperparameter values for a model. It's often done through techniques like grid search, random search, or Bayesian optimization to achieve the highest accuracy possible.

Hypothesis Testing (in AI)

A statistical method for evaluating whether a pattern or relationship found by an AI model is real or due to chance. It helps ensure that model results are meaningful and scientifically valid.

Hybrid Cloud AI

A cloud computing setup that uses both private and public cloud environments to train and deploy AI models. It offers flexibility, scalability, and stronger control over sensitive data.

🔤 AI Glossary — Letter I

Image Recognition

A branch of computer vision that enables AI systems to identify and categorize objects, people, or scenes in images. It's used in facial recognition, medical imaging, self-driving cars, and quality control in manufacturing.

Imbalanced Data

A situation where some classes or categories in a dataset have many more examples than others. Imbalanced data can cause AI models to favor the majority class, leading to inaccurate predictions. Balancing data improves fairness and performance.

Inference Engine

A component of an AI system that applies logical rules or learned patterns to reach conclusions or make decisions. Inference engines are core parts of expert systems and modern language models that generate intelligent responses.

Information Retrieval

The process of searching, extracting, and ranking relevant data from large datasets or documents. AI-powered search engines and chatbots use information retrieval to deliver accurate, context-aware answers.

Input Data

The raw information — such as text, numbers, or images — that an AI system receives before processing. The quality of input data directly affects the reliability of the model's output.

Intelligent Agent

A software entity capable of perceiving its environment, making decisions, and taking actions to achieve specific goals. Examples include virtual assistants, recommendation systems, and AI tutors.

Interpretable AI

An approach to AI design focused on making model decisions understandable to humans. Interpretable AI helps users trust and verify machine-generated outcomes, especially in healthcare, finance, and law.

Iterative Learning

A process where an AI model improves through repeated cycles of training, testing, and refining. Each iteration helps the system learn from its mistakes and perform better over time.

IoT (Internet of Things) AI

AI integrated with smart devices connected through the internet. IoT AI enables objects like thermostats, watches, and appliances to learn user preferences, predict behavior, and operate autonomously.

Isolation Forest

An anomaly detection algorithm that identifies unusual data points by isolating them from the rest of the dataset. It's efficient for spotting fraud, system errors, or rare events.

🔠 AI Glossary — Letter J

Jaccard Index

A statistical measure used to compare the similarity between two sets. In AI and machine learning, it's often used to evaluate clustering or text similarity by dividing the intersection of sets by their union.

Java (in AI)

A programming language often used in AI applications due to its portability, scalability, and strong memory management. Java supports frameworks like Deeplearning4j and Weka, which help in building AI systems for enterprise and academic use.

Joint Embedding

A technique where two or more types of data — such as text and images — are represented in a shared vector space. Joint embeddings allow AI to link visual and textual understanding, as seen in models like CLIP that connect words to images.

JSON (JavaScript Object Notation)

A lightweight data format used for storing and exchanging structured information between systems. AI tools often use JSON to send model inputs, outputs, and metadata in a clear and readable way.

Jump Learning

An advanced learning concept where AI "jumps ahead" in reasoning or skill based on prior knowledge, instead of learning everything from scratch. It mimics human intuition and helps reduce training time in complex models.

🔤 AI Glossary — Letter K

K-Means Clustering

An unsupervised learning algorithm that divides data into *K* distinct groups based on similarity. It assigns each data point to the cluster with the nearest mean value. K-Means is widely used in customer segmentation, image compression, and pattern recognition.

K-Nearest Neighbor (KNN)

A simple yet powerful machine learning algorithm that classifies data based on its proximity to *K* neighboring points. It assumes similar data points are likely to have similar outcomes. KNN is used in recommendation systems and predictive analytics.

Kernel Function

A mathematical function used in Support Vector Machines (SVMs) to transform data into a higher-dimensional space. This allows the AI to separate complex, non-linear data more effectively. Common kernel types include linear, polynomial, and radial basis functions.

Knowledge Base

A structured collection of information that an AI system uses to answer questions, make decisions, or provide explanations. Knowledge bases power systems like virtual assistants, expert systems, and search engines.

Knowledge Graph

A network that connects information through relationships and context, enabling AI systems to understand how data points relate. Knowledge graphs are used by companies like Google to enhance search accuracy and context understanding.

Knowledge Representation

The method of encoding information in a way that AI systems can understand and use for reasoning. It includes logic rules, ontologies, and semantic networks, allowing AI to store and apply knowledge intelligently.

Knowledge Transfer

A technique in AI and machine learning where knowledge gained from one task or dataset is reused in another. This reduces the need for retraining from scratch and speeds up learning in related areas.

Keyword Extraction

A natural language processing technique used to identify the most relevant words or phrases within text. It helps summarize content, improve search results, and enhance AI-driven document classification.

Kinetic AI

A branch of AI that studies movement and motion analysis. It's used in robotics, sports technology, and autonomous vehicles to understand physical actions and predict motion patterns.

Knowledge Distillation

A process where a smaller AI model learns from a larger, more complex model. This helps create faster, lightweight systems that maintain strong performance while using fewer computational resources.

AI Glossary — Letter L

Label Encoding

A data preprocessing technique used to convert categorical (text-based) values into numerical form so that AI models can process them. For example, "Red," "Green," and "Blue" may be encoded as 0, 1, and 2.

Labeled Data

Data that has been tagged with correct answers or classifications, such as images labeled "cat" or "dog." Labeled data is essential for training supervised learning models that rely on known outcomes.

Language Model

An AI system trained to understand, predict, and generate human language. It learns from massive text datasets to perform tasks like translation, summarization, and conversation — examples include GPT and Gemini.

Latent Space

A hidden mathematical representation within an AI model that captures complex relationships between data points. In generative AI, latent space allows systems to create new images, sounds, or text by exploring abstract features.

Lazy Learning

A machine learning approach where the model delays generalization until a prediction is requested. Algorithms like K-Nearest Neighbor (KNN) store data and only compute results when needed, trading speed for flexibility.

Linear Regression

A basic yet powerful algorithm that predicts outcomes by finding the best-fitting straight line through data points. It's commonly used in finance, sales forecasting, and scientific analysis.

Logistic Regression

A classification algorithm used to predict categorical outcomes (like "yes" or "no") instead of continuous values. Despite its name, it's mainly used for probability-based classification rather than regression.

Long Short-Term Memory (LSTM)

A special type of recurrent neural network (RNN) designed to remember long-term dependencies in sequential data, such as language or time series. LSTMs are used in speech recognition, translation, and text generation.

Loss Function

A mathematical formula that measures how far an AI model's predictions are from the correct answers. The goal of training is to minimize this loss, helping the model improve accuracy over time.

Low-Code AI

AI tools that allow users to build and deploy machine learning models with minimal coding. They simplify development for non-programmers, empowering educators, entrepreneurs, and small businesses to use AI effectively.

🔤 AI Glossary — Letter M

Machine Learning (ML)

A core branch of AI where systems learn from data to make predictions or decisions without being explicitly programmed. It powers tools like recommendation engines, fraud detection, and voice recognition.

Meta Learning

Also called "learning to learn," this technique trains AI systems to adapt quickly to new tasks by using prior knowledge. Meta learning helps models generalize better with less training data.

Model Training

The process of teaching an AI model to recognize patterns by feeding it large amounts of data. During training, the model adjusts its internal parameters to minimize errors and improve predictions.

Model Evaluation

A step where an AI model's accuracy and performance are tested using data it hasn't seen before. Evaluation ensures that the model works well in real-world scenarios.

Model Overfitting

A situation where an AI model learns too closely from training data, capturing noise instead of patterns. Overfitting causes poor performance on new data. Regularization and validation help prevent it.

Model Optimization

The process of improving an AI model's efficiency, accuracy, and speed by fine-tuning its architecture, parameters, or algorithms.

Monte Carlo Simulation

A statistical method that uses random sampling to estimate outcomes in uncertain situations. AI systems use it for risk analysis, forecasting, and game simulations.

Multimodal AI

An AI system capable of understanding and processing information from multiple sources — such as text, images, sound, and video — to produce richer and more accurate results.

Multi-Agent System

A group of AI agents that work together or compete to achieve individual or shared goals. They are used in simulations, logistics, and automated trading systems.

Mutation Algorithm

A process inspired by genetics where random changes are introduced to improve AI models' performance during optimization or evolutionary learning.

🔤 AI Glossary — Letter N

Naive Bayes Algorithm

A simple but powerful machine learning algorithm based on probability. It's widely used in spam detection, text classification, and sentiment analysis.

Named Entity Recognition (NER)

An NLP technique that identifies and classifies specific names or entities (like people, places, or organizations) within text.

Natural Language Processing (NLP)

A field of AI that enables machines to understand and respond to human language. It powers chatbots, translation tools, and voice assistants.

Natural Language Understanding (NLU)

A subset of NLP that focuses on interpreting meaning, emotion, and intent behind text or speech. It allows AI to understand context and tone.

Neural Architecture Search (NAS)

An automated method for designing neural networks. AI systems use NAS to discover optimal model structures without human intervention.

Neural Network

A computational model inspired by the human brain, made of layers of nodes (neurons) that process data. Neural networks are the foundation of deep learning systems.

Neuron

Definition

In artificial intelligence and machine learning, a **neuron** (also called a *node* or *unit*) is the fundamental building block of an artificial neural network. It is modeled loosely after the biological neuron found in the human brain. Each artificial neuron receives input signals, processes them mathematically, and produces an output that is passed to other neurons in the network. Neurons collectively enable a model to learn, recognize patterns, and make predictions by adjusting their internal parameters during training.

Key Components

1. **Inputs:**
   The data values or signals that are fed into the neuron — similar to how biological neurons receive signals through dendrites.
2. **Weights:**
   Numerical values assigned to each input that determine their importance. The neuron learns by adjusting these weights during training.
3. **Summation Function:**
   A mathematical operation that combines the weighted inputs into a single value, often using a simple addition or dot product.

4. **Activation Function:**
   A non-linear function (such as ReLU, Sigmoid, or Tanh) applied to the summation result to decide whether the neuron should "fire" or remain inactive.
5. **Output:**
   The final result produced by the neuron after applying the activation function, which becomes the input for other neurons in subsequent layers.

Benefits

- Allows complex relationships to be learned from raw data.
- Enables non-linear transformations for deep learning tasks.
- Builds scalable and flexible structures that can adapt to various problems.
- Mimics the way biological neurons communicate and adapt over time.

Disadvantages

- Individual neurons are simple and limited in function; meaningful behavior arises only when many are connected.
- May become computationally expensive as the network grows deeper.
- Can overfit data if not properly regularized.

Examples

- A neuron in a **convolutional neural network (CNN)** may detect visual patterns such as edges or textures.
- In a **language model**, neurons may learn linguistic features like word order or meaning.
- In **speech recognition**, neurons can capture tone, pitch, and pronunciation patterns.

Applications

- **Image Recognition:** Detecting and classifying objects, faces, or handwriting.
- **Natural Language Processing:** Understanding text, context, and sentiment.
- **Financial Forecasting:** Identifying market trends from numerical data.
- **Medical Diagnosis:** Interpreting scans, patterns, and patient records.

Industries Using Neuron-Based Models

- **Healthcare:** Predictive diagnosis and imaging analysis.
- **Education:** Adaptive learning and student performance prediction.
- **Technology:** AI assistants, chatbots, and autonomous systems.
- **Transportation:** Self-driving cars and sensor-based navigation.

Challenges

- Understanding neuron-level decision-making remains difficult, leading to "black box" behavior.
- Requires large amounts of data and computational resources to train effectively.
- Sensitive to data quality — poor input can lead to unreliable neuron activation.

Summary

A **neuron** is the core unit of intelligence within an artificial neural network. By processing inputs through weighted connections and activation functions, neurons enable machines to simulate learning and reasoning similar to the human brain. Though individually simple, millions of interconnected neurons together form the foundation of modern AI systems, powering technologies from image recognition to natural language understanding.

Node

A basic unit in a neural network that receives input, processes it, and sends it forward. Nodes collectively form layers that learn from data.

Noise (in Data)

Random or irrelevant information in a dataset that can confuse AI models. Removing noise improves accuracy and training efficiency.

Nonlinear Activation

A mathematical function in neural networks that allows models to learn complex, non-straight-line relationships. Common examples include ReLU, Sigmoid, and Tanh functions.

Normalization

A data preprocessing step that scales values into a consistent range to help AI models learn faster and perform better.

AI Glossary — Letter O

Object Detection

A computer vision technique that identifies and locates objects within an image or video. It's used in autonomous driving, security systems, and retail analytics.

Objective Function

A mathematical formula that defines the goal of an AI model — usually to minimize error or maximize accuracy. It guides the learning process during training.

One-Hot Encoding

A method used to represent categorical data numerically by converting each value into a binary vector. It helps AI systems interpret text-based or labeled inputs.

Ontology (in AI)

A structured framework that defines relationships between concepts within a domain. Ontologies help AI organize knowledge logically and reason effectively.

Optimization Algorithm

A method used to adjust model parameters during training to minimize loss and improve accuracy. Examples include Gradient Descent and Adam Optimizer.

Optimization Problem

A task in AI where the goal is to find the best possible solution — like minimizing cost or maximizing performance — under certain constraints.

Outlier Detection

The process of identifying data points that deviate significantly from the rest. Outlier detection helps find errors, fraud, or anomalies.

Overfitting

When an AI model performs well on training data but fails to generalize to new data because it memorized instead of learning patterns.

Overparameterization

A condition where an AI model has more parameters than necessary, often leading to overfitting and inefficiency.

Oversampling

A data balancing technique that increases the number of examples in an underrepresented class to prevent bias during training.

AI Glossary — Letter P

Parameter

A value inside an AI model that determines how it makes predictions. Parameters are adjusted during training to minimize error and improve accuracy.

Pattern Recognition

The ability of AI systems to identify regularities, trends, or structures in data. It's used in handwriting recognition, medical imaging, and speech analysis.

Perceptron

One of the earliest types of artificial neural networks. It consists of a single layer of nodes and is used for simple classification tasks.

Predictive Analytics

A branch of AI that uses statistical models and machine learning to forecast future events based on historical data.

Preprocessing

The preparation of data before feeding it into an AI model — including cleaning, scaling, and encoding — to ensure accuracy and consistency.

Prompt Engineering

The practice of crafting precise and intentional instructions (prompts) to guide AI models in generating accurate and creative responses. It's the foundation of effective human-AI communication.

Probability Distribution

A statistical function that describes the likelihood of different outcomes in a dataset. It's essential for probabilistic reasoning and uncertainty modeling in AI.

Python (Programming Language)

A versatile, easy-to-learn programming language widely used in AI and data science. Python supports major libraries like TensorFlow, PyTorch, and Scikit-learn, making it the most popular tool for AI development.

Pre-trained Model

An AI model that has already been trained on large datasets and can be fine-tuned for specific tasks. Using pre-trained models saves time and computing resources.

Precision and Recall

Two key metrics for evaluating AI performance. **Precision** measures accuracy among positive predictions, while **Recall** measures how many actual positives were correctly identified.

AI Glossary — Letter Q

Q-Learning

A type of reinforcement learning algorithm where an agent learns to make decisions by receiving rewards or penalties. It helps AI systems determine the best action to take in each situation, such as in robotics or game AI.

Quantization

A technique that reduces the precision of numbers in AI models to make them smaller and faster without major loss in accuracy. It's commonly used to optimize models for mobile or edge devices.

Quantum AI

The integration of quantum computing and artificial intelligence. Quantum AI uses the principles of quantum mechanics to process complex computations faster than traditional computers.

Query

A request for information sent to a database or AI system. In natural language models, queries are user inputs — the "questions" that trigger responses.

Queue Learning

A data-handling strategy where information is processed sequentially, one at a time. It's useful for managing AI tasks or workflows that must follow a specific order.

AI Glossary — Letter R

Random Forest

An ensemble learning algorithm that combines multiple decision trees to improve accuracy and reduce overfitting. It's used for both classification and regression tasks.

Recurrent Neural Network (RNN)

A neural network designed for sequential data such as text, speech, or time series. RNNs have loops that allow them to "remember" previous inputs, making them ideal for language and forecasting tasks.

Regression Analysis

A statistical method that models the relationship between variables to predict future outcomes. Linear and logistic regression are common types.

Reinforcement Learning

An AI learning method where an agent interacts with its environment and learns from feedback through rewards and penalties. It's used in robotics, gaming, and automation.

Representation Learning

A machine learning technique where the system automatically discovers useful features from raw data instead of relying on manual feature selection.

Retrieval-Augmented Generation (RAG)

A model that combines information retrieval and text generation. It fetches relevant data before producing a response, improving accuracy in AI question-answering systems.

Reward Function

A key component of reinforcement learning that defines how much "reward" an AI receives for taking certain actions. It guides the system toward desirable outcomes.

Robotic Process Automation (RPA)

Technology that uses AI to automate repetitive digital tasks, such as data entry or document processing, to increase efficiency and reduce human error.

Rule-Based System

An AI system that makes decisions based on predefined rules or conditions, often used in expert systems or early AI programs.

Runtime Environment

The system or platform where AI models are executed. It includes the software, hardware, and configurations required for the model to function properly.

🔤 AI Glossary — Letter S

Scalability

The ability of an AI system to handle increasing amounts of data or users without losing performance. Scalable AI models grow with business and computational needs.

Semi-Supervised Learning

A learning method that combines a small amount of labeled data with a large amount of unlabeled data to improve model performance.

Sentiment Analysis

A natural language processing technique that identifies emotions or opinions in text, such as positive, negative, or neutral sentiment. It's used in marketing and social media monitoring.

Signal Processing

The analysis and transformation of data signals (like sound, images, or time series) into meaningful patterns. AI uses it in speech recognition and medical imaging.

Speech Recognition

A technology that converts spoken language into text using AI models trained on voice data. It powers virtual assistants and transcription tools.

Supervised Learning

A machine learning technique where a model is trained using labeled data, meaning both inputs and correct outputs are provided during training.

Swarm Intelligence

An AI concept inspired by nature, where simple agents (like ants or bees) collectively solve complex problems. It's used in optimization, robotics, and network routing.

8. Symbolic AI

An early AI approach based on logical rules and symbolic representations. Unlike modern machine learning, it uses explicit reasoning rather than pattern recognition.

Synthetic Data

Artificially generated data created to train AI models when real data is limited or sensitive. It helps improve privacy and expand datasets.

AI Glossary — Letter T

Target Variable

The specific outcome or label that an AI model aims to predict, such as "spam or not spam" or "disease present or absent."

TensorFlow

An open-source AI framework developed by Google that helps developers build and train machine learning models efficiently.

Token Limit

The maximum number of tokens (words or symbols) an AI model can process in a single interaction or context window

Tokenization

The process of breaking text into smaller units, or "tokens," such as words or subwords, to help AI models understand language.

Transfer Learning

A technique where a model pre-trained on one task is adapted to a different but related task, saving time and improving performance.

Transformer Architecture

Definition

Transformer Architecture is a deep learning model framework introduced in 2017 by Vaswani et al. in the paper *"Attention Is All You Need."* It revolutionized natural language processing (NLP) by replacing traditional sequence models like RNNs (Recurrent Neural Networks) and LSTMs (Long Short-Term Memory networks) with a mechanism known as **self-attention**, allowing the model to understand relationships between words or elements in a sequence — regardless of their distance from each other.

Key Components

1. **Encoder-Decoder Structure:**
   The architecture typically has two main parts — the encoder, which reads and represents the input data, and the decoder, which generates the output based on the encoded information.
2. **Self-Attention Mechanism:**
   This mechanism lets the model weigh the importance of each word relative to others in a sentence, improving context understanding.
3. **Multi-Head Attention:**
   Multiple attention layers run in parallel, enabling the model to capture different kinds of relationships or meanings simultaneously.
4. **Positional Encoding:**
   Since Transformers do not process data sequentially, positional encodings are added to indicate the order of elements in a sentence.
5. **Feed-Forward Networks:**
   After attention layers, fully connected neural networks help the model transform and refine the contextual representations.
6. **Residual Connections and Layer Normalization:**
   These ensure stability during training and help the model learn complex patterns efficiently.

Benefits

- Handles long-range dependencies more effectively than RNNs.
- Enables parallel processing, making it faster to train on large datasets.
- Produces state-of-the-art performance across multiple tasks, such as translation, summarization, and text generation.
- Scales well to massive datasets and larger models like GPT, BERT, and T5.

Disadvantages

- Extremely data- and computation-intensive, requiring powerful hardware.
- Can be prone to bias if trained on unbalanced or low-quality datasets.

- Difficult to interpret because of its complexity and multi-layered attention mechanisms.

Applications

- **Natural Language Processing (NLP):** Machine translation, text summarization, sentiment analysis, and chatbots.
- **Vision Transformers (ViTs):** Image recognition and object detection in computer vision.
- **Speech Recognition:** Improved context-aware transcription and voice command systems.
- **Multimodal AI:** Combining text, images, and audio for generative and reasoning tasks.

Industries Using Transformer Models

- **Technology:** Google, OpenAI, Meta, and Microsoft for large-scale AI systems.
- **Education:** Intelligent tutoring systems and adaptive learning platforms.
- **Healthcare:** Medical data analysis and clinical text interpretation.
- **Entertainment:** Script generation, gaming narratives, and subtitles translation.

Challenges

- High energy consumption during training and inference.
- Potential for producing inaccurate or biased outputs if the model is not fine-tuned properly.
- Data privacy concerns in large-scale, open-domain training environments.

Summary

The Transformer Architecture represents a fundamental shift in how machines understand and generate language. Its self-attention mechanism allows models to process context more globally and flexibly than ever before. Transformers laid the foundation for today's most advanced AI systems — including ChatGPT, BERT, and countless others — marking a turning point in modern artificial intelligence.

Transformer Model

A neural network architecture that processes sequences of data (like text) more efficiently than traditional RNNs. It's the foundation of modern large language models such as GPT.

Training Data

The dataset used to teach an AI model. Training data must be diverse and accurate to ensure reliable model performance.

Turing Test

A test developed by Alan Turing to evaluate whether a machine can exhibit intelligent behavior indistinguishable from that of a human.

Time Series Analysis

The use of AI to analyze sequential data over time, such as stock prices or weather patterns, to forecast future trends.

Tunable Parameters

Adjustable values in an AI model that influence its performance, such as learning rate or layer depth. Tuning helps achieve optimal results.

🔤 AI Glossary — Letter U

Unlabeled Data

Data that has not been tagged with specific outputs or categories. It's commonly used in unsupervised and semi-supervised learning.

Unstructured Data

Information that doesn't follow a predefined format, such as text, images, videos, or social media posts. AI tools process it using natural language and computer vision techniques.

Unsupervised Learning

A machine learning method where models learn from unlabeled data to find patterns, groupings, or hidden structures without specific instructions.

Uncertainty Modeling

The process of estimating how confident an AI model is about its predictions. It helps improve trust and decision-making in sensitive domains like medicine or finance.

Update Rate

The frequency at which an AI model adjusts its parameters during training. A balanced update rate ensures faster learning without instability.

User Intent Recognition

An NLP technique that determines the purpose or goal behind a user's input — essential in chatbots and voice assistants for accurate responses.

Utility Function

A mathematical function used in AI to evaluate the desirability or usefulness of different actions. It's often used in decision-making and reinforcement learning.

🔤 AI Glossary — Letter V

Validation Set

A portion of the dataset used during model training to fine-tune parameters and prevent overfitting. It helps evaluate how well the model generalizes to unseen data before final testing.

Value Function (in Reinforcement Learning)

A function that estimates the expected reward an AI agent will receive from a certain state or action. It guides decision-making by helping the agent choose actions that maximize long-term rewards.

Variance (in AI Models)

A measure of how much a model's predictions change when trained on different data samples. High variance means the model is sensitive to noise and may overfit.

Vectorization

The process of converting data (like text or images) into numerical vectors that AI models can process. It's essential in natural language processing and computer vision.

Verification (in AI Systems)

The process of checking whether an AI model or system performs its intended function correctly and safely before deployment.

Virtual Agent

An AI-driven digital assistant designed to interact with humans through voice or text. Examples include chatbots, customer service bots, and AI tutors.

Virtual Reality (VR)

A computer-generated environment that simulates real or imagined worlds. When combined with AI, VR can create adaptive, interactive learning and training experiences.

Vision Transformer (ViT)

A deep learning model that applies transformer architecture — originally used for language — to image recognition tasks. It divides images into patches and processes them like words in a sentence.

Voice Recognition

AI technology that identifies and processes human voices to perform tasks, such as unlocking devices or activating voice assistants.

Volumetric Data

Three-dimensional data used in fields like medical imaging, 3D modeling, and geoscience. AI uses it to analyze structures and visualize depth in complex environments.

🔤 AI Glossary — Letter W

Weak AI (Narrow AI)

AI designed to perform a specific task, such as translation or image classification. It does not possess general reasoning or consciousness like humans.

Weight (in Neural Networks)

A numerical value that determines the strength of a connection between neurons. During training, weights are adjusted to reduce prediction errors.

Weighted Average

A statistical method that assigns different importance (weights) to data points when calculating an average. AI uses it to prioritize more relevant or reliable data.

Whisper Model

An AI model developed by OpenAI for automatic speech recognition (ASR). It transcribes and translates spoken language into text across multiple languages with high accuracy.

Wi-Fi Sensing AI

Technology that uses Wi-Fi signals to detect movement or monitor environments without cameras. It's used in security, healthcare, and smart homes.

Windowing Function

A mathematical function used in signal processing and speech recognition to divide data into smaller segments for analysis.

Word Embedding

A representation of words in numerical form where similar words are placed close together in vector space. It helps AI models understand semantic relationships in text.

Word2Vec

A popular algorithm for creating word embeddings by learning relationships between words based on their context within large text datasets.

Workflow Automation

The use of AI to streamline repetitive business tasks such as approvals, document sorting, and scheduling. It increases productivity and reduces human error.

World Model (in AI)

A conceptual model an AI system builds to understand and predict the behavior of the environment around it — especially in robotics and autonomous systems.

🔠 AI Glossary — Letter X

XAI (Explainable AI)

A field of AI focused on making models transparent and understandable to humans. It explains how decisions are made, which builds trust and accountability.

XGBoost (Extreme Gradient Boosting)

A powerful machine learning algorithm known for its high performance in classification and regression tasks. It's widely used in data science competitions and predictive modeling.

XML (Extensible Markup Language)

A structured text format used to store and share data between systems. AI applications use XML for configuration, annotations, and data exchange.

XOR Problem

A classic logic problem that early neural networks struggled to solve. It led to the development of multilayer neural networks capable of learning non-linear relationships.

🔠 AI Glossary — Letter Y

YAML (YAML Ain't Markup Language)

A human-readable data format often used for AI configuration files, datasets, and machine learning pipelines. It's easy to read and integrates well with Python-based AI frameworks.

YOLO (You Only Look Once)

A fast real-time object detection algorithm that identifies and locates multiple objects in a single pass. It's widely used in autonomous vehicles and security systems.

Yield Prediction AI

AI systems that forecast agricultural output based on environmental data, crop type, and soil conditions. It supports smarter farming and food sustainability.

Yearly Seasonality Model

A model used in time-series forecasting that accounts for repeating annual patterns — such as sales spikes or weather cycles — to improve accuracy.

🔠 AI Glossary — Letter Z

Zero-Shot Learning

An AI method that allows a model to recognize new objects or tasks it has never seen before by using prior knowledge or contextual reasoning.

Zettabyte

A unit of digital storage equal to one sextillion (10^{21}) bytes. AI models and data centers increasingly operate with zettabyte-scale data due to massive global information growth.

Z-Score Normalization

A statistical technique used to standardize data by subtracting the mean and dividing by the standard deviation. It helps machine learning models handle data with different scales.

Zone-Based AI

A decision-making approach where an AI system divides its environment into regions or "zones" for localized reasoning and optimized control — used in robotics and traffic management.

Zoom Out Learning

A training strategy where AI is encouraged to look at problems from broader perspectives rather than narrow details, improving reasoning and generalization.

What to Say When You Talk to AI — Puzzle Pack

Puzzle 1: Word Search — The Language of Prompts

Instructions:
Find each term below in the grid (forward, backward, diagonal). Circle them as you go.

Words to Find:
PROMPT CONTEXT SYSTEM USER TONE CONSTRAINTS EXAMPLES TOKENS SAFETY ITERATE MEMORY GUARDRAILS CHAIN CRITIQUE

G	U	A	R	D	R	A	I	L	S	E	Q
R	T	O	K	E	N	S	A	F	E	T	Y
I	C	O	N	T	E	X	T	M	E	M	O
T	P	R	O	M	P	T	R	O	S	Y	S
I	U	S	E	R	I	T	E	R	A	T	E
Q	T	O	N	E	X	A	M	P	L	E	S
U	C	H	A	I	N	O	C	R	I	T	I
E	N	S	T	R	A	I	N	T	S	M	Y
S	Y	S	T	E	M	T	O	K	E	N	S
E	X	A	M	P	L	E	S	T	O	N	E
M	E	M	O	R	Y	S	A	F	E	T	Y
C	O	N	T	E	X	T	G	U	A	R	D
R	A	I	L	S	P	R	O	M	P	T	U
I	T	E	R	A	T	E	U	S	E	R	N

PUZZLE 2

CROSSWORD GRID (blank for readers to fill in)

1 2 3 4 5 6 7 8 9 10 11 12

----

1 |_|_|_|_|_|_| | | | | | |

2| | |_| | | | | | | | | |

3 |_|_|_|_|_|_|_| | | | | |

4| | |_| | | | | | | | | |

5 |_|_|_|_|_|_| | | | | | |

6| | |_| | | | | | | | | |

7 |_|_|_|_|_|_| | | | | | |

8| | | | | | | | | | | | |

9 |_|_|_|_| | | | | | | | |

10| | |_| | | | | | | | | |

11| _|_|_|_|_| | | | | | | |

12| | | | | | | | | | | | |

CLUES

Across

1. The message you give to an AI to make it respond (6 letters).
2. The background or situation you include to help AI understand better (7 letters).
3. The structure or engine that processes your request (6 letters).
4. Units that measure the length of text in AI systems (6 letters).
5. The person or agent giving the instruction to AI (4 letters).
6. A linked series of thoughts or operations — like "chain of thought" (5 letters).

Down

1. A method that helps AI reason step-by-step (5 letters).
2. The tone or mood you want the AI to use (4 letters).
3. The protective rules built to prevent harmful outputs (10 letters).
4. When AI repeats or refines based on your feedback (7 letters).
5. Short examples that teach the AI what kind of answer you expect (8 letters).
6. The memory mechanism that helps AI remember past inputs (6 letters).

ANSWER KEY (for teacher or back of book)

Across:
PROMPT CONTEXT SYSTEM TOKENS USER CHAIN

Down:
REACT TONE GUARDRAILS ITERATE EXAMPLES MEMORY

🗣 PUZZLE 3: PROMPT MAD LIBS — "Design Your Own Prompt"

Fill in each blank, then read your complete prompt aloud.
Would the AI understand you clearly?

1. **Goal:** I want the AI to ______________________________________.
2. **Audience & Tone:** Speak to _____________________________ in a _________ tone.
3. **Context:** Here is the background in one sentence: __________________________________.
4. **Constraints:** Must include _____________________________ and exclude ___________________________.
5. **Format:** Return the answer as a(n) ________________________ with _________ bullets / steps.
6. **Quality Bar:** A great answer would include ____.

🎯 **Bonus Exercise:**
Now rewrite your answers into one strong, complete prompt using this pattern:

[Role] + [Goal] + [Audience / Tone] + [Context] + [Constraints] + [Format] + [Quality Bar].

🔎ANSWER KEY

Puzzle 1: Secret Message
→ THINK CLEAR BEFORE YOU PROMPT

Puzzle 2: Cryptoquote Solution
→ Be clear when you talk to AI, be kind too!

Puzzle 3: Prompt Mad Libs
→ Answers will vary. A great prompt is clear, specific, and purposeful.

Index

Epilogue: The Conversation That Never Ends

When I first began exploring the world of AI, I didn't imagine it would lead to this — not just a book, but a movement in how we think, create, and communicate.

At its core, this book was never about technology alone. It was about *connection.*
Every prompt, every question, every line of dialogue is a reflection of our deepest human curiosity — the desire to understand and to be understood.

AI is not replacing that desire; it's amplifying it.
It gives us a mirror that reflects our imagination, our reasoning, and our values in real time. And like any meaningful relationship, what we receive depends entirely on what we bring to the conversation.

The art of prompting is really the art of thinking out loud — with clarity, intention, and empathy.
It asks us to slow down, to articulate our ideas more thoughtfully, and to recognize how powerful words can be when they are guided by vision.
Each prompt you write is a seed of thought planted into an infinite field of knowledge.
What grows depends on the care, precision, and creativity you give it.

You are not just using AI — you are shaping it.
With every conversation, you are teaching it how humans dream, reason, and feel. You are defining what intelligent collaboration looks like in the 21st century.

The future will not be written by machines alone.
It will be co-authored — by you, by me, and by every curious mind willing to ask better questions.
And that's the true message of this book: **when you learn what to say when you talk to AI, you also learn more about what it means to be human.**

So as you close this final page, don't think of it as an ending.
It's just the beginning of a lifelong dialogue — one that grows smarter, kinder, and more creative with every word you choose to share.

Keep asking.
Keep imagining.
Keep the conversation alive.

Because the future doesn't just answer our questions — it listens.

Author's Note

Writing *What to Say When You Talk to AI* has been one of the most rewarding journeys of my life.
This book was born from countless conversations — not just with artificial intelligence, but with myself, my readers, and the future we are all stepping into together.

I wrote this guide because I believe that everyone — teachers, students, creators, entrepreneurs, and dreamers — deserves to understand how to talk to AI with confidence and creativity. The truth is, prompting is not a technical skill reserved for programmers. It's a human skill — the skill of thinking clearly, communicating effectively, and expressing curiosity in a way that inspires intelligent response.

Through this process, I discovered that the real magic of AI isn't in its data or algorithms. It's in the *dialogue* — the moment a human question meets a machine's understanding. That's where learning, creativity, and progress begin.

This is my sixth book, and with each one, I've learned something new about the power of language and the power of faith in possibility. From building websites and writing educational resources to creating this guide on AI communication, one lesson remains constant: when you ask with intention, life — and now technology — responds with opportunity.

If this book helped you speak more clearly with AI, think more deeply about your ideas, or feel more confident in this new digital era, then it has fulfilled its purpose.

Thank you for joining me on this journey.
Keep exploring, keep asking, and keep believing that your words can shape intelligence — because they truly can.

With gratitude and inspiration,
Susie Hala
Author & Creator of *The AI Dictionary Series*

KO E 'OTUA MO TONGA KO HOKU TOFI'A
TONGA

alamy

www.ingramcontent.com/pod-product-compliance
Ingram Content Group UK Ltd.
Pitfield, Milton Keynes, MK11 3LW, UK
UKHW062012041026
15591UKWH00017B/1301